LIFE WITHOUT ME
DANIEL KEENE

CURRENCY PRESS
SYDNEY

MTC
MELBOURNE
THEATRE
COMPANY

CURRENCY PLAYS

First published in 2010
by Currency Press Pty Ltd,
PO Box 2287, Strawberry Hills, NSW, 2012, Australia
enquiries@currency.com.au
www.currency.com.au
in association with
Melbourne Theatre Company

NATIONAL LIBRARY OF AUSTRALIA CIP DATA

Author:	Keene, Daniel, 1955–.
Title:	Life without me / Daniel Keene.
ISBN:	9780868198927 (pbk.)
Subject:	Australian drama.
Dewey Number:	A822.3

Typeset by Dean Nottle for Currency Press.
Cover photograph by Earl Carter.
Cover design by Lydia Baic.

Contents

Currency Press acknowledges the Traditional Owners of the Country on which we live and work. We pay our respects to all Aboriginal and Torres Strait Islander Elders, past and present.

In our most trivial walks, we are constantly, though unconsciously, steering like pilots by certain well-known beacons and headlands, and if we go beyond our usual course we still carry in our minds the bearing of some neighbouring cape; and not till we are completely lost, or turned round—for a man needs only to be turned round once with his eyes shut in this world to be lost—do we appreciate the vastness and strangeness of nature. Every man has to learn the points of compass again as often as he awakes, whether from sleep or any abstraction. Not till we are lost, in other words not till we have lost the world, do we begin to find ourselves, and realize where we are and the infinite extent of our relations.

Henry David Thoreau
Walden, *Chapter Eight*

for
Monica Maughan

Life Without Me was first produced by Melbourne Theatre Company at the Sumner Theatre, Melbourne, on 14 October 2010, with the following cast:

NIGEL	Robert Menzies
JOHN	Greg Stone
ROY WILLIAMS	Brian Lipson
ALICE JARVIE	Deidre Rubenstein
MRS SPENCE	Kerry Walker
TOM	Benedict Hardie
ELLEN	Kristina Brew

Director, Peter Evans
Set and Costume Designer, Dale Ferguson
Lighting Designer, Matt Scott
Composer, Jethro Woodward
Assistant Director, Matt Scholten

The Melbourne Theatre Company production of *Life Without Me* was produced in association with the Melbourne International Arts Festival.

MELBOURNE
INTERNATIONAL
ARTS FESTIVAL

CHARACTERS

NIGEL, hotel clerk, about 40
JOHN, a hotel guest, about 50
ROY WILLIAMS, a salesman, late 50s
ALICE JARVIE, a guest, mid 50s
MRS SPENCE, Nigel's mother, about 70
TOM, a guest, mid 30s
ELLEN, his wife, mid 30s

SETTING

The lobby of a two-star hotel. The place has seen better days.

At rear, centre, an elevator. To the elevator's right, the door to the stairs. Mid stage left, the entrance (a revolving door); either side of the entrance, a couple of battered sofas, side tables, table lamps. Mid stage right, the check-in desk; behind the desk, the door to the office. A large fish tank downstage of the desk. Front of stage, left of centre, a grouping of three armchairs and a coffee table.

Above the lobby, left and right, the small balconies of two of the hotel's rooms.

All directions are given from the viewpoint of the audience.

Note: if an interval is desired, it should follow Scene Three.

SCENE ONE

Evening.

Darkness.

The sound of thunder, howling wind and rain, the crackle of lightning.

Lights rise to reveal NIGEL *standing by the fish tank, gazing into the empty water. After a few moments he moves slowly to the revolving door and looks out briefly. He turns away and moves to behind the desk. He takes the register from under the desk and opens it. He slowly runs his finger down the page, reading. He closes the register and puts it back under the desk. He moves from behind the desk and approaches the elevator. He is about to press the button when a light bulb above the desk expires with a soft 'pop'.* NIGEL *moves back to the desk and looks up at the bulb. He turns and goes into the office. He returns with a fresh bulb. He climbs up onto the desk to remove the expired bulb. He isn't quite tall enough to reach the light fitting; he stands on his toes, teetering on the brink of falling.*

An enormous crash of thunder rattles the building. NIGEL *falls, landing behind the desk with a sickening thud; at the same time, the revolving door spins open in a blast of wind. Refuse and dead leaves blow wildly across the lobby, followed by* JOHN, *who is literally blown through the door, his overcoat soaking wet, his umbrella turned inside out. He carries a small suitcase.*

The revolving door stops spinning. JOHN *stands dripping, breathless. He lowers his umbrella and tries to close it, as* NIGEL *slowly emerges from behind the desk, looking dazed, a trickle of blood running from the bridge of his nose. He sees* JOHN.

The storm outside gradually begins to ease and die away throughout the following.

NIGEL: That's very bad luck.

      JOHN *looks up, startled.*

  An open umbrella indoors is bad luck.

JOHN: [*still struggling with the umbrella*] I know.

NIGEL: Then could you please close it?

JOHN: You're bleeding.

NIGEL: I fell.

JOHN: Are you alright?

NIGEL: I don't know.

> JOHN *finally manages to close his umbrella.*

Can I help you with something?

JOHN: Do you have a room?

NIGEL: We have a lot of rooms.

> JOHN *approaches the desk.*

JOHN: Do you have a vacant room?

NIGEL: Quite a number.

JOHN: Could I have one?

NIGEL: Just for tonight?

JOHN: I'm not sure yet.

> NIGEL *reaches under the desk and fetches a large tissue; he dabs at the blood on his nose.*

NIGEL: Do you have a reservation?

JOHN: No.

NIGEL: You thought you'd just turn up…

JOHN: Is that a problem?

NIGEL: Not for me. But most people make arrangements. They reserve a room.

JOHN: I haven't, so can I—?

NIGEL: How do you manage?

JOHN: Pardon?

NIGEL: Just drifting from place to place…

JOHN: Excuse me?

NIGEL: … hoping you'll be able to find a room.

JOHN: I don't drift from place to—

NIGEL: Because there are times when I'd have to tell you that we don't have a room available, we're booked up, full.

JOHN: Are you?

NIGEL: No, not at the moment.

JOHN: So I can have a room.

NIGEL: What kind of room would you like?

JOHN: I want a room with a bed in it.

NIGEL: They all have beds.

JOHN: So any room will do.

NIGEL: Do you want a room with a view?

JOHN: Of what?

NIGEL: You can have a room with a view of the front of the building on the opposite side of the street or you can have a room with a view out the back of the building.

JOHN: What's out the back of the building?

NIGEL: The back of another building.

JOHN: I see. Then I'll have—

NIGEL: Of course there are rooms on either side of the building whose windows face the sides of other buildings.

JOHN: Fine. I'll have—

NIGEL: Or you can have a room with no view at all.

JOHN: No view at all?

NIGEL: Nothing.

JOHN: Aren't there any windows?

NIGEL: There are windows in all our rooms. At least one window per room.

JOHN: So there must be a view.

NIGEL: Not necessarily.

JOHN: If you look out of a window… you see something.

NIGEL: Yes, you might see something, but you might not necessarily describe what you see as a view.

JOHN: What would you describe it as?

NIGEL: No idea really.

> JOHN *takes off his dripping overcoat.*

JOHN: Is there somewhere that I could hang this?

NIGEL: You can hang it in your room.

JOHN: I don't have a room, yet.

NIGEL: No.

JOHN *folds his overcoat and lays it on top of his suitcase.*

JOHN: These rooms with no view… what do you see when you look out the window?

NIGEL: Another window in this building.

JOHN: Pardon?

NIGEL: It's the way the building's built. You see, in the centre of this building is a… I'm not sure what you'd call it. I suppose you could call it a shaft.

JOHN: A ventilation shaft?

NIGEL: Are you an architect?

JOHN: No.

NIGEL: Oh. Anyway, the rooms in the centre of this building have windows that look out onto this shaft. And across the other side of the shaft are… other windows looking out onto the shaft.

JOHN: That's a view of something.

NIGEL: I don't think that a view of the building that you're actually in counts as a view. A view, for my money, has to be of something else, of another building, at least, otherwise you're not—

JOHN: I'll have one of those… with a view of the ventilation shaft.

NIGEL: Sorry, they're all taken.

JOHN: All of them?

NIGEL: They're very popular.

Pause.

JOHN: What rooms are available?

NIGEL: There are several. Front, back and side.

JOHN: One at the front.

Pause.

NIGEL: You're shivering.

JOHN: I'm cold. I'm wet through.

NIGEL: I thought that you might be ill.

JOHN: I probably will be. These rooms at the front…

NIGEL: If you take a room at the front you'll be woken very early on account of the traffic. It gets very noisy.

JOHN: I'll have a room at the back then.

NIGEL: There's no sun back there, no light at all. Very gloomy.

JOHN: If you were staying here, what room would you choose?

NIGEL: Here? I wouldn't stay here.

JOHN: Where would you stay? Perhaps I'll go there.

NIGEL: You don't know what you want, do you?

JOHN: It's late, I'm tired. I want a room.

　　　NIGEL *checks his watch.*

NIGEL: It's only eight o'clock.

JOHN: Could I just have a room? I don't give a rat's arse which one.

NIGEL: There's no need to get aggravated.

JOHN: But you're aggravating me.

NIGEL: I find that hard to believe.

JOHN: I'm telling you that you are.

NIGEL: I would have thought just the opposite.

JOHN: What, that you're being helpful?

NIGEL: Helpful isn't the opposite of aggravating.

JOHN: What is?

NIGEL: What am I, a thesaurus?

JOHN: I just want a room. This is a hotel, isn't it?

　　　Pause.

NIGEL: You came in here not knowing whether or not it was a hotel?

JOHN: Of course I knew it was a hotel.

NIGEL: Then I don't understand your question.

JOHN: It was rhetorical.

NIGEL: I see.

JOHN: I'll have a room at the front, I like to wake up early.

NIGEL: That's entirely up to you. [*He produces the register and turns it to face* JOHN.] Name and details there. Payment is in advance.

JOHN: Do you have a pen?

NIGEL: Not at the moment.

JOHN: But—

NIGEL: Do you have one?

JOHN: I might have.

> JOHN *searches through his pockets.*

NIGEL: I usually carry a pen on me.

JOHN: But not tonight?

NIGEL: I didn't mean at work. I don't carry a pen at work.

JOHN: I would have thought it might be useful.

NIGEL: Well, if you can't find one it would be.

> JOHN *pulls a pencil from his jacket pocket.*

JOHN: I've got a pencil.

NIGEL: A pencil…

JOHN: Will that do?

NIGEL: Something written in pencil can be erased.

JOHN: But—

NIGEL: You write your details in the register… [*shutting the register*] and when I open it in the morning… [*opening the register*] they're gone. Erased.

JOHN: Who… who would erase them?

NIGEL: It would be as if you were never here, as if you never existed.

JOHN: [*sotto*] Oh, for God's sake… [*Pause.*] What if I press hard, so that the pencil leaves an indentation? Then if someone erases my details during the night, we can still read them.

NIGEL: It'd be very difficult in this light. You see [*looking up*] I was just about to put in a new light bulb when you—

JOHN: We could rub it, we could rub the side of the pencil, [*demonstrating*] rub the lead of the pencil, over the indentation, and that way read what was written there.

NIGEL: Could we?

JOHN: The indentation itself wouldn't be coloured by the lead, but the paper around the indentation would, so that the words I'd written and had been erased would appear as white letters. It would be… like a negative of what I'd written.

NIGEL: How do you know all this?

JOHN: All what?

NIGEL: All these things about indentations and rubbing?

JOHN: I used to do it when I was a kid. It was a kind of game.

NIGEL: Shall we try it?

JOHN: What?

NIGEL: Write down your details, we'll erase them, then do that thing you said.

JOHN: Do we have to?

NIGEL: We need to establish whether or not this theory of yours holds up.

JOHN: It's not a theory.

NIGEL: To me it is.

JOHN: Alright, alright, I don't intend to argue about it.

NIGEL: But you are rather argumentative.

JOHN: I'm not, usually.

NIGEL: You seem to be.

JOHN: Look, if we do establish that my 'theory' holds up…?

NIGEL: Then a pencil will be a perfectly adequate instrument with which to record your details as we have the means to recover them if they are erased.

JOHN *sighs and writes.* NIGEL *watches him.*

Are you pressing?

JOHN: I am. [*Pause.*] There. Done.

NIGEL: Do you have an eraser?

JOHN: No.

NIGEL: But you have a pencil.

JOHN: That doesn't mean—

NIGEL: I would have thought that you would therefore have an eraser.

JOHN: Do you?

NIGEL: Why would I have—?

JOHN: Could you look? Maybe there's one behind the desk somewhere.

NIGEL: There's nothing behind the desk. Just me. [*Pause.*] So…

They both look down at the register.

We're a bit stuck.

JOHN: What do you mean?

NIGEL: Well, in the first place, you've written your details in pencil, which, strictly speaking, isn't really acceptable. In the second place, because we have no way of—

JOHN: Forget about it, I'll go elsewhere. I should have gone elsewhere before I was blown in here. Goodnight.

JOHN *picks up his overcoat and suitcase.*

NIGEL: There's no need to be hasty.

JOHN: I think there is.

JOHN *turns and heads for the door.*

NIGEL: You're a very agitated kind of person, aren't you?

JOHN *stops.*

I've seen it before, time and time again.

JOHN *turns back to* NIGEL.

JOHN: I wonder why that is?

NIGEL: It's the way things are nowadays. People are very agitated.

JOHN *and* NIGEL *look at one another.* JOHN *approaches the desk.*

JOHN: Have we gotten anywhere? About my room?

NIGEL: I'm not sure.

JOHN *moves away from the desk and sits in one of the armchairs.*

NIGEL *comes out from behind the desk; he approaches* JOHN.

There are two kinds of people who come in here. Those that know where they are, where they've been and where they're going, and those… that don't. I'm a very keen observer of people. I've seen people come in here who are in all kinds of trouble.

JOHN: What kinds of trouble?

NIGEL: I could tell you things.

JOHN: I'm sure you could.

NIGEL *sits in one of the armchairs near* JOHN.

NIGEL: But discretion is my rule.

JOHN: That's very admirable, I'm sure. [*Pause.*] Tell me… do I look like a man in trouble?

NIGEL: What kind of trouble?

JOHN: The kind of trouble that a man like me could get into.

NIGEL: I don't know what kind of man you are.

JOHN: Hopeless but far from desperate. [*He stands up and spreads his arms.*] Take a look at me. Take a really good look. [*Pause.*] What do you think? Say anything you like, I can take it.

NIGEL: I really don't—

JOHN: I'll bet you've seen some desperate characters.

NIGEL: Now and then.

> JOHN *starts pacing around the lobby.*

JOHN: If I seem agitated it's because I am. I'm actually very agitated. I'm agitated because I've been trying to leave this city for three days… but I can't. I've been wandering the streets, day and night, searching for a way out. But I can't find one.

> *He turns to* NIGEL, *who makes no response.*

I've lived here in this city all my life. But three days ago I decided to leave it and never come back. I won't explain why.

NIGEL: Please don't.

JOHN: But it seems that I can't… actually leave. I can't find the train station. I can't find the bus terminal. I can't seem to hail a taxi. I've asked for directions and I've been given them, but those directions always lead me back to where I started. I haven't slept in three days. I've eaten at certain establishments, each one cheaper and dirtier than the last. I've been going around in smaller and meaner circles. [*Pause.*] I can't get out. [*Pause.*] I don't know what's happening. But something is happening. Something is thwarting me.

> NIGEL *stands and returns to the desk.* JOHN *follows him.*

There was a moment, yesterday afternoon at about four o'clock, a moment when I thought that I was going mad. But I'm not going mad. If you're going mad, do you think that you're going mad? No. You don't. You just go mad. And that's it, you're… kaput. [*He looks despairingly around the lobby.*] I didn't mean to come here. I was blown in here by the wind.

NIGEL *is suddenly very businesslike; he checks the register.*

NIGEL: I can give you front single. Seventy-five dollars. [*He opens a drawer behind the desk, finds a room key.*] Check-out is at ten in the morning. I'll need to know by then whether you intend to stay another night.

JOHN: I've left no-one behind. There are no loved ones involved. I live alone. That's the way I've chosen to live. A life lit by my own lights. A quiet bed. An empty morning. A silent homecoming. What's wrong with a man alone, if not happy then content with his lot, if not content then at least accepting, if not accepting, then at least resigned, if not resigned, then at least… without hope?

NIGEL *holds out the room key.*

NIGEL: Room 304, third floor. [*He puts the key down on top of the desk.*] Seventy-five dollars. Cash.

JOHN *takes out his wallet, opens it and hands over the money.*

NIGEL *pockets the cash.*

JOHN *takes the key.*

JOHN: Thank you.

JOHN *picks up his overcoat and suitcase and moves towards the elevator.*

NIGEL: I'm afraid that the elevator's out of order.

JOHN *presses the button.*

The elevator doors open with a bright 'ting'.

JOHN *steps inside, smiling.*

JOHN: Goodnight.

The elevator doors begin to close.

JOHN *waves.*

The elevator doors shut.

NIGEL *turns the register to read John's details; he runs his fingers over John's entry. The pencil is lying between the open pages.*

NIGEL *picks up the pencil and puts it in the breast pocket of his shirt.*

Above, we hear the elevator arrive at the third floor; the doors open with a bright 'ting'.

NIGEL *looks up.*

We hear John's footsteps as he steps out of the elevator and walks along the hallway. He reaches his room; we hear his key turning in the lock. The door opens; the door shuts.

NIGEL *looks down and shuts the register as the lights fade to black.*

SCENE TWO

Morning.

The crow of cock, bark of dogs, bright twitter of birds, blare of traffic, then sudden silence.

Lights rise on the lobby.

NIGEL *is asleep on a sofa by the entrance, curled up inside a sleeping bag; he is quite invisible.*

After a few beats, we hear footsteps descending the stairs. The door to the stairs opens and JOHN *enters the lobby. He goes immediately to the elevator and pushes the button. The elevator doors open with a bright 'ting'. He stares into the elevator for a few moments, puzzled. He reaches inside the elevator and pushes the button to close the doors. The doors close. He walks away from the elevator, passes the check-in desk and stands staring at the empty fish tank. He leans close to the tank and taps on the glass; there is no sign of life. He taps again, leaning closer, his forehead touching the glass.*

A middle-aged man in a dark suit, ROY WILLIAMS, *struggles through the front door, stooped under the weight of the two large suitcases he carries. He walks straight to the desk and puts down the suitcases. He straightens up, easing his back, takes a handkerchief from his pocket and mops his brow.*

JOHN *watches him for a moment, then slowly approaches.*

JOHN: Excuse me… Tony? Is that you… Tony?

ROY: [*turning to* JOHN] I'm sorry?

JOHN: Tony Burke?

They stand looking at one another.

ROY: I'm sorry but I—

JOHN: No, I'm sorry. I thought you were someone I know… someone I used to know. An old friend of mine.

ROY: Oh, I see. That's perfectly understandable. I've often been mistaken for someone else.

JOHN: Who?

ROY: Pardon?

JOHN: Who have you often been mistaken for?

ROY: I haven't always been mistaken for the same person, I didn't mean that. I've been mistaken for lots of different people. I have that kind of face.

JOHN: What kind of face?

ROY: People think I'm someone else. I could be anybody.

JOHN: We could all be anybody.

ROY: How do you mean?

JOHN: Do you know who I am?

ROY: No, I don't.

JOHN: So I could be anybody.

ROY: But I don't think that you're someone that you're not. Even if I don't know who you are I don't think that you're someone else, I mean someone that I know, whereas you did mistake me for someone that you know.

JOHN: Sure, that's true, but—

ROY: I just have the kind of face that reminds people of someone else. [*He cranes his neck to look through the office door.*] Is there anyone—?

JOHN: What kind of face would you say I have?

ROY: [*turning back to* JOHN] You have your own face, perfectly your own. I seem to have lots of people's faces. I'm generic, I suppose.

JOHN: I wouldn't say so.

ROY: The person I reminded you of… does he actually look like me?

JOHN: Well, now that you ask, not particularly.

ROY: And yet you thought I was him. What is it about my face that made you think that?

JOHN: I can't say really.

ROY: I have the kind of face that people take in with a single glance. There's nothing about it that requires any thought, nothing to distinguish it from a hundred other faces. My face has no character.

JOHN: I wouldn't say that.

ROY: Whereas your face has character. Your life has left its mark. My life on the other hand has left my face untouched. Of course I've aged, I didn't look like this twenty years ago, but those twenty years have left no trace. My face doesn't... speak. My face is silent.

JOHN: What does my face say?

ROY: Oh, loads of things.

JOHN: What?

ROY: I'm not sure I should tell you.

JOHN: That bad, eh?

ROY: Whatever I'd say would only be my opinion. The important thing is that your face is your face. I couldn't have mistaken you for anyone. Yours is a face that I don't know. That's the important thing.

JOHN: Of course, yes, I can see that.

ROY: People are a fascination of mine. Strangers, I mean. Of course, my fascination is quite specific. One might even say it's myopic. I can stand on a crowded railway platform but what I see is only one person, usually the most nondescript... a middle-aged man tying his shoelace, or a woman reading a newspaper, her glasses slightly skewed, her lipstick smudged, a tired, resigned look about her. Her hands look cold, perhaps they're trembling. She's going home from work. Sometimes I might imagine what she's going home to. But what I imagine her life to be is probably far from the truth. What I imagine about her is an imposition. She'll never be aware of it, but... I've committed a kind of crime against her. I've imagined her life based on the little evidence I have of it, I've turned something real into something imagined. That seems innocent enough. But is it?

JOHN: I don't know.

ROY: I don't either. I try to keep my thoughts and imaginings to myself…
but I can't seem to.

JOHN: You do talk a lot.

ROY: Yes, I do. It's a terrible habit of mine.

An awkward pause.

JOHN: I'd still like to know what you see when you look at me. What does
my face say?

ROY: Oh, loads and loads of things.

JOHN: Tell me.

Pause.

ROY: Well… if you'd like. [*He looks, closely, directly into* JOHN*'s face.*]
Shut your eyes. Please.

JOHN: Okay.

JOHN *closes his eyes;* ROY *moves a little closer.*

ROY: When your eyes are shut your face reveals more. The best faces to
look at are sleeping faces. A sleeping face looks innocent, no matter
whose face it is.

JOHN: I feel quite uncomfortable.

ROY: That's understandable.

JOHN: So, can I—?

ROY: Your face is like a closed door. It's been closed very slowly. No-one
noticed it happening, not even you. And now the key is turning, to
lock it up for good.

JOHN *opens his eyes.*

JOHN: Thanks. I think that's enough.

JOHN *turns and walks away.*

ROY: I'm sorry.

JOHN: Don't be. I asked you to tell me what you saw.

ROY: I'm not sorry for what I said.

JOHN *turns back to him.*

JOHN: You don't have any right to be sorry for me. I'll be alright. I've always been alright. So don't be sorry for me.

> JOHN *has returned to the fish tank; he peers in and taps on the glass.*

> ROY *looks in through the office door.*

ROY: Is there anyone… is the manager in, do you know?

JOHN: I don't think this place has a manager. [*He taps on the glass again.*] Nothing…

> NIGEL *stirs and wakes and appears out of the top of his sleeping bag; he sees* JOHN *tapping on the glass.*

NIGEL: Don't you know that you should never tap on a fish tank? That tapping on the glass sends shock waves through the water that can kill a fish stone dead.

JOHN: Where are the fish?

NIGEL: There aren't any.

JOHN: So what does it matter if I tap on the glass?

> NIGEL *unzips his sleeping bag and gets up; apart from his shoes, he is fully dressed. He rolls up the bag and drops it behind the sofa.*

NIGEL: You do it once, you do it twice and before you know it, it's become a habit. You won't be able to help yourself. Everywhere you go you'll leave a trail of dead fish in your wake.

JOHN: I don't think I will, actually.

> NIGEL *slips on his shoes, which he takes from under the sofa, and walks behind the desk.*

NIGEL: [*to* ROY] How can I help you?

> ROY *offers his hand;* NIGEL *ignores it.*

ROY: Roy Williams. I'm here about the linen.

NIGEL: The linen?

ROY: I rang last week. I was in the area last week and I thought that I might drop in. But it wasn't a convenient time.

NIGEL: Wasn't it?

ROY: So you said. At least, I presume it was you.

NIGEL: I don't recall.

ROY: I have an appointment with the owner of the hotel, Mrs Spence. I've brought the samples to show her. Apparently your bed linen is in a shocking state.

NIGEL: I wouldn't say that.

ROY: But you did say it, when I called last week.

JOHN: I'd say it was.

NIGEL: [*ignoring* JOHN] Are you sure you were speaking to me?

ROY: Is there anyone else I could have been speaking to?

NIGEL: No, not really.

JOHN *has wandered over to the sofa and glances behind it.*

JOHN: Do you sleep down here every night?

NIGEL: I slept here last night.

JOHN: Is it a regular thing?

NIGEL: Where I sleep is my business.

JOHN: Why don't you sleep in one of the rooms?

NIGEL: I have to be down here in case I'm needed.

JOHN: By whom?

NIGEL: It's my job.

JOHN: But—

ROY *has taken a large diary from one of his suitcases and flicks through the pages.*

ROY: I made an appointment to speak to the owner of the hotel.

He holds up the diary and shows NIGEL *an open page.*

It's right here.

NIGEL: Where?

ROY: [*pointing at the page*] There. My appointment.

NIGEL: But it isn't.

ROY: What?

ROY *spins the diary around and looks at the page: it's blank.*

NIGEL: Perhaps you wrote it in invisible ink?

ROY *stares at the page.*

ROY: I made an appointment with the owner, Mrs Spence…

NIGEL: The owner isn't in today. Mrs Spence is never here on a Thursday.

ROY: I made an appointment…

ROY *flicks through the pages of the diary.*

NIGEL: But you didn't.

JOHN *approaches the desk.*

JOHN: There's something wrong with the elevator, by the way.

NIGEL: I know. I told you there was.

JOHN: I went up in the elevator last night.

NIGEL: Yes.

JOHN: But this morning when I wanted to come down… nothing happened.

NIGEL: It's out of order.

ROY *slaps the diary shut.*

ROY: This is very inconvenient for me. Appointments are made to be kept.

NIGEL: There is no appointment.

ROY: I might have forgotten to write it down. Perhaps you have it written down somewhere?

JOHN: He doesn't have a pen.

ROY: [*turning to* JOHN] Excuse me?

JOHN: He doesn't have a pen, not at work.

ROY: It's taken me an hour and a half to get here on public transport, do you know what public transport's like in this city? It'd be quicker getting about on a penny farthing. Do you know how heavy these sample cases are?

JOHN: You look exhausted.

ROY: Exhausted? [*He moves to one of the armchairs and slumps into it.*] Sometimes I think that I've been exhausted my whole life.

JOHN: How do you deal with it?

ROY: I don't.

JOHN: You don't have a car? I would have thought—

ROY: I had a car. I don't have one now. My son ran it into a tree two weeks ago.

JOHN: Is he okay?

ROY: No, he's an idiot.

> NIGEL *has opened the register.*

NIGEL: [*to* JOHN] Excuse me… will you be staying another night?

JOHN: Are they still there?

NIGEL: Are what still there?

JOHN: My name and details. They haven't been erased?

NIGEL: No.

JOHN: That's a relief. [*He goes to the desk.*] Do you know a place where I could get some breakfast?

NIGEL: How hungry are you?

JOHN: Does that make a difference?

NIGEL: I was going to fix something for myself and there's no reason why I couldn't do you a couple of eggs on toast as well.

JOHN: You're being very obliging.

NIGEL: That'll pass, it's early in the day.

JOHN: I don't want to put you out.

NIGEL: It'll cost you ten dollars.

JOHN: For eggs on toast?

NIGEL: And coffee. Instant.

JOHN: Perhaps it might be best if I went to a café…

> *Pause.*

NIGEL: Make up your mind. I'm hungry.

JOHN: Okay, I'll take the eggs on toast. Where's the dining room?

> JOHN *opens his wallet and hands over the money for breakfast;*
> NIGEL *pockets the cash.*

NIGEL: There isn't one. You can eat down here or in your room.

JOHN: What about the kitchen?

NIGEL: There's no kitchen. I've got everything I need in the office.

JOHN: Can we eat in the office?

NIGEL: It's very small. Why do you think I was sleeping out here? If the office was big enough, I'd sleep in the office.

JOHN: I suppose you would.

NIGEL: How do you like your eggs? I can do fried or scrambled.

JOHN: I'd prefer poached.

NIGEL: Poaching an egg is a mystery to me. I've never been able to do it.

JOHN: I could do it myself, I don't mind.

NIGEL: I can't let guests into the office.

JOHN: Not even to poach an egg?

NIGEL: I can't.

JOHN: Fried then.

NIGEL: Take a seat, I won't be long.

> NIGEL *turns to go into the office.*

> JOHN *looks over at* ROY, *who seems to have dozed off.*

JOHN: What about him?

NIGEL: [*glancing at* ROY] What about him?

JOHN: He could probably do with something as well.

NIGEL: Three breakfasts? I don't know if I can manage. I have limited facilities.

> JOHN *has gone over to* ROY *and shakes him gently by the shoulder.*

JOHN: Do you want some breakfast?

ROY: [*waking, a little dazed*] What?

JOHN: Have some breakfast.

ROY: I've had breakfast.

JOHN: Do you like eggs?

ROY: Yes, I like eggs.

JOHN: You've had a long trip, a disappointment, you're tired. Have some eggs.

ROY: I'm actually a bit… a bit short of cash at the moment.

JOHN: It'll be on me.

NIGEL: [*waiting, impatiently*] What's it to be?

JOHN: [*to* ROY] Fried or scrambled eggs?

ROY: I like poached eggs.

JOHN: He can't do poached.

ROY: Fried?

NIGEL: Have we made up our minds?

JOHN: [*going to the desk*] He'll have fried as well.

> *He takes out his wallet and pays for Roy's breakfast.*
>
> NIGEL *pockets the cash, turns and goes into the office.*
>
> JOHN *moves back to* ROY *and sits in one of the armchairs.*

ROY: Thank you that's very kind of you.

JOHN: No trouble.

ROY: I am a little hungry. I set off quite early this morning. It seems like a week ago. And it seems the day's going to be a complete loss… again. I was hoping to make a sale today. It needn't have been a large one. Just something to tide me over. I don't have any other appointments.

JOHN: Business is a bit slow?

ROY: I've never known it so bad, and I've been selling sheets and pillowcases for thirty years. I can tell you the thread count of a cotton sheet just by touching it. [*He holds out his hands and looks at them.*] My hands are old. [*He smiles briefly at* JOHN.] Thirty years ago I was the same man. I was a different man as well, of course. I'm that same different man. I don't really understand that. [*Pause.*] I keep expecting to meet myself, in a doorway somewhere, sitting at the back of the bus, standing at a bar… falling from a high window. I have this constant expectation. I don't think it's healthy. I'm a mystery to myself. But it's a mystery that I'm used to and that I'm bored with. A man can't live like that. But that's how I've lived. [*He gets up from the armchair and walks over to the empty fish tank; he taps on the glass.*] The passing of time is cruel. There's no appeal to be made, there's no-one who'll listen or who'll care. Time's cruel. [*He stares into the fish tank.*] There's absolutely nothing in here.

> *The elevator doors open with a bright 'ting'.*
>
> ALICE JARVIE *steps out of the elevator. She carries a large potted palm. She is wearing a scarf that covers her mouth and nose.*
>
> *The elevator doors close behind her. She struggles with the plant*

towards the desk, soil spilling from the pot, where she places it on top of one of Roy's suitcases.

ROY *sees what she's done and moves towards her.*

I'm sorry, excuse me…

ALICE *takes no notice. She reaches behind the desk and searches around; she finds a counter bell. She puts the bell on top of the desk and rings it several times.*

Could you please take that plant off my suitcase?

NIGEL *comes out of the office.*

NIGEL: Who did that? That bell's hotel property.

ALICE *pulls off her scarf.*

ALICE: I don't want that plant in my room.

ROY *takes the plant off his case and puts it on the desk.*

NIGEL: [*to* ROY] Don't do that.

ALICE: I'm allergic to it, terribly allergic.

ROY: I've got samples in that case.

NIGEL *takes hold of the plant and moves it from the desk to beside the elevator.*

ALICE *follows him.*

ALICE: I woke up during the night—

ROY: Look, there's dirt all over the case.

ALICE: I was in a shocking state.

ROY: That case is company property.

ALICE: I didn't know what was happening to me.

NIGEL *moves back behind the desk.* ALICE *follows him.*

I was being… asphyxiated, that's how bad it was. Are you listening to me?

NIGEL: I seem to be.

ALICE: My breath came in huge gasps… in huge, horrible gasps. [*She gasps, hugely.*] I sat up in the darkness and told myself not to panic. I don't believe in panic. It's counterproductive in my opinion.

NIGEL: I agree.

ALICE: Then I turned and I saw it, I saw it… lurking by the window, waving its… fronds, like some deformed… hand…

JOHN *has moved to the elevator. He pushes the button. The elevator doors open with a bright 'ting'. He steps inside and pushes a button. The doors remain open. He pushes the button again. Nothing happens.*

I got out of bed and approached it… gasping. [*She gasps.*] I got hold of it, I don't know how I did it, but I did, and I put it outside the door. Eventually my breathing returned to normal. It was a nightmare. I've had hardly any sleep at all. And my nightie is covered in soil.

NIGEL: [*unmoved*] I've never had any complaints before.

ALICE: [*pointing to the plant*] That thing is poisonous. It belongs in the jungle, not in a decent person's room.

She holds her scarf to her mouth and nose.

ROY *has been staring at* ALICE. *He steps a little closer to her.*

ROY: Alice?

ALICE: [*turning to him*] I beg your pardon?

NIGEL *looks at* JOHN.

NIGEL: I told you it's out of order.

JOHN: Not all the time.

ROY: Alice. It's me, Roy.

ALICE *slowly lowers her scarf.*

ALICE: Roy? I don't believe it…

Dark smoke has begun to drift from the office doorway.

JOHN: [*to* NIGEL, *pointing*] I think you're needed in the office.

NIGEL *turns and sees the smoke.*

NIGEL: Shit, the toast!

NIGEL *rushes into the office.*

As JOHN *watches him, the elevator doors slowly close.*

ALICE *is staring at* ROY's *face.*

ALICE: I didn't recognise you.

> *They gaze at one another, then suddenly embrace.*
>
> *We hear the fire extinguisher gushing in the office as the lights fade to black.*

SCENE THREE

Lights rise on the lobby.

Noon.

A little smoke might still be drifting in the air.

The lobby is empty for a few beats.

*A couple enter (*TOM *and* ELLEN*); they each carry a small suitcase.*

They wait at the desk for a few moments; TOM *kisses* ELLEN*'s cheek.*

ELLEN: Don't.
TOM: Don't what?

> *He kisses her cheek again.*

ELLEN: Don't do that.
TOM: Why?
ELLEN: Because I say so.

> ELLEN *rings the bell; there is no response.*
>
> TOM *kisses her cheek again.*

Why are you such an idiot?
TOM: I can't help myself.
ELLEN: Perhaps we should find someone who can.

> *She rings the bell again; there is no response.*
>
> TOM*'s attention has been drawn to the elevator; he moves to it.*

TOM: Did you hear that?
ELLEN: What?

> *She joins* TOM *by the elevator.*

TOM: Listen…

They both lean close to the elevator; a muffled voice can be heard.

ELLEN: [*her face close to the door*] Hello… hello…?

The voice grows louder, but is still incomprehensible.

Perhaps if we…

She pushes the button.

The elevator doors open with a bright 'ting'.

JOHN *stumbles out of the elevator, dishevelled and out of breath.*

JOHN: Thank Christ!

TOM *and* ELLEN *back away.*

I've been in there for hours. [*He sniffs the air.*] God, you can still smell that smoke.

ELLEN: What smoke?

JOHN: Do you have a reservation?

TOM: Yes… and no.

ELLEN: What smoke?

TOM: Do you work here?

JOHN: No. But the clerk can get very difficult if you don't have a reservation.

ELLEN: We have a reservation, but not at this hotel.

JOHN: Pardon?

TOM: We have a reservation at another hotel, but the taxi dropped us off here…

ELLEN: It was our mistake really. About this smoke…

TOM: We don't know the city very well.

ELLEN: We're from interstate.

TOM: And we'd been driving around for quite a while.

ELLEN: We were pretty lost actually.

JOHN: Oh dear…

ELLEN: What smoke?

JOHN: Toast. It was toast.

TOM: It was the driver's first day on the job, so he said.

JOHN: You don't say…

ELLEN: We just liked the look of this place. What toast?

TOM: All hotels are pretty much the same… in our price range, I mean.

JOHN: I'd say this place was fairly unique.

ELLEN: How so?

JOHN: You'll find out.

TOM: Do you like it here?

JOHN: Oh, yes. It's a laugh a minute here.

TOM: Did someone recommend it to you?

JOHN: No. I was just… blown in through the door.

TOM: Are you from interstate?

JOHN: No. I live in this city. I'm trying not to live here anymore, but I can't seem to manage it.

>   ELLEN *has moved to the fish tank and is tapping on the glass.*

Don't do that. It can kill a fish, doing that.

ELLEN: But there aren't any fish.

JOHN: That's exactly what I said.

TOM: To who?

JOHN: You'll meet him.

>   ELLEN *has returned to the desk and rings the bell several times.*

TOM: I don't think anyone's there.

>   ELLEN *goes behind the desk and is about to enter the office when* NIGEL *appears in the doorway. He carries a paintbrush; paint is spattered on his clothes.*

NIGEL: Will you please stop ringing that bell. [*He grabs the bell and tosses it under the desk.*] What are you doing back here? This is a restricted area.

JOHN: I've been trapped in the elevator.

NIGEL: Whose fault it that?

ELLEN: You should put a sign on it.

JOHN: Are you saying it's my fault?

NIGEL: You stepped into it.

TOM: It really should have a sign if it's out of order.

NIGEL: What good would a sign do? I tell people to their face that the elevator's out of order but they still use it.

JOHN: It works sometimes.

NIGEL: It's unpredictable. An elevator goes up and it goes down, it goes up, it goes down. If it stops doing either of those things it is out of order.

ELLEN: Are you going to have it fixed?

NIGEL: Not right now.

JOHN: Why not?

> NIGEL *gestures with the paintbrush.*

NIGEL: I've had to clean up the mess from the fire extinguisher, and now I'm painting the wall above the toaster which was damaged during… the incident.

TOM: What incident?

> NIGEL *has spattered paint over* ELLEN.

ELLEN: You idiot! Look what you've done.

TOM: You'll have to pay to have that cleaned.

NIGEL: Have you seen my shirt? Who's going to pay for my shirt to be cleaned?

ELLEN: This is a very expensive dress.

NIGEL: If you had done as I asked and stepped out from behind the desk it wouldn't have happened.

ELLEN: But it has happened.

NIGEL: Why am I suddenly responsible for everything?

JOHN: It's your hotel.

NIGEL: It is not my hotel. I am an employee of the hotel. My responsibilities are limited.

JOHN: To what exactly?

> ELLEN *has come from behind the desk and stands beside* TOM.

NIGEL: What do you two want anyway?

TOM: We'd like a room.

NIGEL: Do you have a reservation?

ELLEN: No.

NIGEL *reaches under the desk, finds the register and slams it down.
Pause.*

TOM: Do you have a pen?

NIGEL: No.

The lights suddenly fade to black.

Above the lobby, lights rise on the balcony, left.

ALICE *is dabbing her eyes with a handkerchief.* ROY *stands at her
shoulder.*

ROY: I'm terribly sorry.

ALICE: So am I. And a little embarrassed.

ROY: It was more my fault than yours.

ALICE: It was an honest mistake, neither of us are to blame really.

An awkward pause.

ROY: It's actually quite funny.

ALICE: Yes. Very funny. In a way.

Pause.

ROY: But you did know a Roy, and I knew an Alice.

ALICE: Yes, I did. And you did. But we're not them.

ROY: No.

ALICE: No, we're not.

Pause.

ROY: It would be quite strange if we were really.

ALICE: Pardon?

ROY: If we did meet, if we were who we thought we were, I mean who
we thought we were down in the lobby, if you were who I thought
you were and I was who you thought I was.

ALICE: I suppose it would.

ROY: What would be the chances of meeting again, after more than thirty
years, I mean meeting just by chance like that? It would be unusual.

ALICE: Yes, it would.

ROY: But we haven't. I mean we haven't really met, I mean again.

ALICE: No. It would be too much of a coincidence if we were who we thought we were.

Another awkward pause.

ROY: I'm here on business. At least I thought that I was. But it turns out that I'm not. So I'm here for no reason at all. What about you?

ALICE: I'm waiting. I sold my old apartment a while ago and my new place was supposed to be ready by now, but it's not, of course. There have been problems, delays with the building. Do you know the French phrase *'la salle des pas perdus'*?

ROY: I'm sorry, but French is all Greek to me.

ALICE: It can mean 'the room of lost steps', something like a waiting room, a train station, a place between one place and another, between leaving and arriving, where nothing can really happen.

Pause.

ROY: Of course there is a coincidence, you know, in our meeting. Your name is Alice and mine is Roy, even if you're not the Alice I thought you were.

ALICE: And you're not my Roy. [*Pause.*] I shouldn't say that. He's not my Roy anymore. He never was, really. If he had been he still would be. But that's just how I like to remember him.

Pause.

ROY: Sometimes remembering is like wishing, remembering things that we wish had been true.

ALICE: There's not much point in that, is there?

ROY: Does there have to be? [*Pause.*] I knew a young woman named Alice. I knew her when I was a young man. I thought that I'd forgotten her. But then I saw you and I thought that you were her and... all of a sudden I knew how much I'd missed her, how I'd missed her terribly.

Pause.

ALICE: Do I look very much like her?

ROY: Only a little, really. Around the eyes. She used to do what you were doing... she'd hold her scarf up to her face on cold days, she hated the cold on her lips.

ALICE: It was because you said your name that I thought you were him. It's an old-fashioned name. You don't hear it much anymore. [*Pause.*] So… now we've met. We're strangers. Should we stay that way?

ROY: No, I don't think we should.

ALICE: Then tell me about yourself.

ROY: I'm a salesman, once quite successful, but not anymore. I've been a widower for more than ten years now. I have a grown son, who I love dearly but who drives me to distraction. I'm almost sixty years old and I'm at the end of my rope. And I'm very pleased to have met you.

The lights fade on ROY *and* ALICE.

In the darkness:

VOICE: [*off*] Hello! Hello! It's me… Mummy's here!

The lights rise on the lobby.

MRS SPENCE *enters through the revolving door. She wears a hat and coat. She carries a clear plastic bag in each hand; in the bags, water and several goldfish.*

MRS SPENCE: Hello… I'm here!

NIGEL *comes out of the office, wiping his hands on a towel. He stops behind the desk.*

NIGEL: What are you doing here?

MRS SPENCE: I've brought the fish.

NIGEL: It's Thursday.

MRS SPENCE: Is it?

NIGEL: You don't come in on a Thursday. What fish?

Pause.

MRS SPENCE: Isn't that peculiar…

NIGEL: What?

MRS SPENCE: Well, I didn't really mean to come in.

NIGEL: Yet here you are.

MRS SPENCE: That's what's peculiar. I had no intention of coming here at all. Yet as you say, here I am. I do wonder sometimes what I get up to. It's often a complete mystery to me.

NIGEL: Join the club.

MRS SPENCE: What day do I come in?

NIGEL: When I ask you to.

MRS SPENCE: When do you ask me?

NIGEL: I don't.

He comes out from behind the desk.

MRS SPENCE: You're being very obscure, Nigel. Help me with these fish. I think they're unwell.

NIGEL: What's wrong with them?

MRS SPENCE: We have had a very long journey and the weather is quite unpleasant. Fish, as you should know, are sensitive creatures.

NIGEL: Why should I know that?

MRS SPENCE: You are not a stupid boy, Nigel, I've seen to that. While there are certain areas in which you remain untutored, your grasp of general knowledge, as I remember, is admirable.

NIGEL: I don't know anything about fish.

MRS SPENCE: Every man on the street knows something about fish.

NIGEL: I find that hard to believe.

She thrusts the plastic bags at him.

MRS SPENCE: Here, take them, they are now your responsibility.

NIGEL: Do they have to be?

MRS SPENCE: I've done my duty, now do yours. I'm worn out.

He reluctantly takes the fish.

MRS SPENCE *sits on one of the sofas.*

You had your own goldfish when you were a little boy. Do you remember?

NIGEL: Vaguely.

MRS SPENCE: You loved that fish. You called him Mr Shakespeare.

NIGEL: Did I?

MRS SPENCE: Yes. You were very literate when you were young. I don't know what's happened to you.

NIGEL: I'm still literate.

MRS SPENCE: But not in the same way. You're more… peculiar in your tastes now.

NIGEL: My tastes are my own.

MRS SPENCE: That's what worries me.

> NIGEL *goes to the fish tank and places the two plastic bags on the surface of the water.*

What are you doing?

NIGEL: I'm putting the fish in the tank.

MRS SPENCE: I think it would be better if you removed them from their plastic bags, so they can actually be in the water. It's their natural habitat.

NIGEL: They'll die if I do that.

MRS SPENCE: But Nigel… they're fish.

NIGEL: The temperature of the water in the bag is different than the temperature of the water in the tank. If I released the fish straight into the water they would probably die of shock, having no time to adjust to the different temperature. But by resting the bags in the water, the water in the bags will gradually match the temperature of the water in the tank. When the water in the bags is the same temperature as the water in the tank, then I can safely release the fish.

MRS SPENCE: See, you do know about fish. You're very clever. I can't wait to tell your father. He's always said that you're clever, even when you've shown no evidence of it.

> *Pause.*

NIGEL: Mum…

MRS SPENCE: Have you seen him lately?

NIGEL: No, I haven't.

MRS SPENCE: It's very odd for him to go missing for so long. Of course, he's always gone missing, ever since I first met him. He'd go off and I'd never know when he'd turn up again. It was always such a wonderful surprise when he did.

NIGEL: It'd certainly be a surprise if he turned up now.

MRS SPENCE: I haven't seen him for ages and ages.

NIGEL *sits next to his mother on the sofa.*

NIGEL: You won't be seeing him, Mum. We've talked about this before.

MRS SPENCE: About what?

NIGEL: About Dad.

MRS SPENCE: What about him?

NIGEL: He's gone, Mum.

MRS SPENCE: I can't stand waiting for him if I don't know where he is. When we were younger it didn't matter. He'd go off and I'd be quite happy to wait for him without knowing where he'd got to. But now I don't like waiting for him if I can't imagine where he is, if I can't picture some place and him in it. So if you know where he is, you have to tell me. I don't care how long he's gone but I need to know where he is.

Pause.

NIGEL: Dad passed away.

Pause.

MRS SPENCE: Don't be ridiculous. I'd know if he passed away.

NIGEL: One would have thought so.

MRS SPENCE: The passing away of a person, a lovely person like your father, someone very dear to those who knew him and loved him… [*her voice beginning to trail off*] the passing away of such a dear man… [*Pause.*] He was very old, wasn't he?

NIGEL: Yes, Mum, quite a few years older than you.

Pause.

MRS SPENCE: He needed to wander, you see. [*Pause.*] I don't really forget that he's gone. But I like to forget. The trouble is of course that sometimes… sometimes I want to forget so very badly… that I think I actually do. It's very confusing.

NIGEL: It must be.

Pause.

MRS SPENCE: Sometimes I wish that what I know I only wish to be true was actually true. Does that make sense?

NIGEL: Probably, Mum, probably.

Pause.

MRS SPENCE: He needed to wander, and perhaps I do too, in my own way. People are very strange, aren't they?

NIGEL: Some are less strange than others.

MRS SPENCE: I think that all people are strange, it's just that some hide it better than others. Your father couldn't hide it. I loved him for it. Although it did make my life... a little odd.

NIGEL: Mine too, Mum.

MRS SPENCE: You don't resent him for that, do you?

NIGEL: I never had the chance to resent him. I was just... bewildered by him.

MRS SPENCE: Do you remember when he developed a habit of appearing in other people's photographs? [*She laughs at the memory of it.*] If he saw a wedding, or even a funeral, or tourists posing in a group in front of some landmark, he'd find a way into the picture. He was the man on the edge of the gathering that no-one knew. He liked to imagine the puzzled looks on people's faces when the photograph was developed. He'd imagine himself being cut out with a pair of scissors, or folded under the edge of the picture frame when it was hung on the wall. Somehow that pleased him... the fact that he'd been where he shouldn't have been. That always pleased him. [*Pause.*] I never understood why. [*Pause.*] I miss him.

NIGEL: I know.

MRS SPENCE: I knew his face so well. I knew his face when he was sleeping, I knew the rhythm of his breath. I knew his eyes closing at night and when they first opened in the morning. And he knew mine... [*Pause.*] But he's not here anymore... and I am.

NIGEL: God, I just remembered.

MRS SPENCE: What?

NIGEL: I told someone that you wouldn't be here today.

MRS SPENCE: Who?

NIGEL: It doesn't matter. A man.

MRS SPENCE: Why did you tell him that?

NIGEL: Because you're not supposed to be here.

MRS SPENCE: Why is he here?

NIGEL: It doesn't matter. I don't want to deal with it.

MRS SPENCE: He must be here for a reason.

NIGEL: He is. But you're not here. Alright?

MRS SPENCE: But, dear, I am here. Anyone can see that.

NIGEL: You could go.

MRS SPENCE: I've just arrived, and I told you I'm worn out. I'd love a cup of tea.

NIGEL: Well, if this chap comes down you just act like a guest.

MRS SPENCE: How do I do that?

NIGEL: Go up to your room or something.

MRS SPENCE: But I don't have a room.

> *He goes to the desk, reaches under it, finds a key, comes back to his mother and hands it to her.*

NIGEL: Here, room 302, that can be your room. You can have a proper rest, a lie-down. I'll bring you a cup of tea.

MRS SPENCE: I hope you're not making a habit of giving rooms away for free.

NIGEL: Mum, this is your hotel, you can stay in any room you like any time you like.

MRS SPENCE: Why would I do that?

NIGEL: If the occasion arises.

MRS SPENCE: I'm perfectly happy at home. I don't need to stay in a hotel.

NIGEL: I know that.

MRS SPENCE: I've never liked staying in hotels.

NIGEL: I know.

MRS SPENCE: I certainly wouldn't stay in this hotel.

NIGEL: Not many people do.

MRS SPENCE: How many guests do we have at the moment?

NIGEL: Quite a few, quite enough.

MRS SPENCE: How many?

NIGEL: Four.

> *Pause.*

MRS SPENCE: Doesn't it put them off?

NIGEL: What?

MRS SPENCE: Staying in an empty hotel.

NIGEL: No-one's mentioned it.

MRS SPENCE: We have eighteen rooms. If only four of them are occupied—

NIGEL: Three rooms are occupied. Two singles and a double.

MRS SPENCE: And no-one's said anything?

NIGEL: I keep them in the dark as much as possible.

MRS SPENCE: How do you do that?

NIGEL: I lie to them.

MRS SPENCE: Nigel…

NIGEL: And… [*He goes back to the desk and produces the register.*] I fill this with names and details. Take a look. Would you suspect that most of the signatures on this page have been written by the same person?

> MRS SPENCE *comes over to the desk and examines the signatures.*

I've developed at least twelve different hands.

MRS SPENCE: So you've become a forger.

NIGEL: Only in the interests of our guests. They feel more comfortable about staying here if they think that quite a number of other people have chosen to as well.

MRS SPENCE: But quite a number of other people haven't.

NIGEL: No.

MRS SPENCE: The place must feel quite… empty.

NIGEL: I move around quite a bit, at night, from floor to floor, flushing the occasional toilet.

MRS SPENCE: My poor dear, you must be exhausted.

NIGEL: I haven't been home in six months. I've rented my flat to a couple of foreign exchange students.

MRS SPENCE: Are they decent?

NIGEL: Information Technology.

MRS SPENCE: Well, I suppose that's fairly hygienic. [*She moves away from the desk and sits in one of the armchairs.*] I'm not sure that I'm entirely happy with these arrangements, Nigel.

NIGEL: It's the best I can do.

> *Pause.*

MRS SPENCE: Is there any hope?

NIGEL: Of what?

MRS SPENCE: Of business improving.

NIGEL: I haven't given that possibility much consideration.

> *The elevator doors open with a bright 'ting'.*

> JOHN *steps out.*

Are you still playing around with that thing?

JOHN: I couldn't resist.

NIGEL: You should show a little more restraint.

JOHN: I like to live dangerously.

NIGEL: I won't be held responsible.

JOHN: Responsible is not a word I'd associate with you.

> *He looks across at* MRS SPENCE *and nods a greeting.*

Hello.

MRS SPENCE: I'm not here.

JOHN: Sorry?

MRS SPENCE: I'm not here. I'm in room 302.

> *She holds up her key.*

> JOHN *takes his key from his pocket and holds it up.*

JOHN: I'm in 304.

MRS SPENCE: We're practically neighbours.

NIGEL: Is there something I can help you with?

JOHN: [*turning to* NIGEL] I'll be staying another night.

NIGEL: You were supposed to tell me that this morning.

JOHN: I was in the elevator all morning.

MRS SPENCE: What were you doing in the elevator?

JOHN: Paying for my sins.

MRS SPENCE: I'm not religious.

JOHN: [*turning to* MRS SPENCE] Neither am I. I find that much certainty discouraging.

NIGEL: That's seventy-five dollars.

JOHN *gets out his wallet and takes out the cash.*

MRS SPENCE *approaches the desk.*

MRS SPENCE: Nigel…

She gestures for NIGEL *to come closer.*

He leans towards her.

[*Behind her hand*] Is this the chap?

NIGEL: Chap?

MRS SPENCE: Who mustn't know I'm here.

NIGEL: No, but just to be on the safe side…

MRS SPENCE: [*winking*] I understand.

NIGEL *turns back to* JOHN, *who hands him the money;* NIGEL *pockets the cash.*

Nigel…

She gestures for him to come closer.

He leans towards her again.

NIGEL: Yes… madam.

MRS SPENCE: [*quietly*] Do you think I could have some of that money, for a taxi home? I spent my last money on the fish.

NIGEL *turns his back to* JOHN *and hands a twenty-dollar note to his mother.*

JOHN *wanders over to the fish tank; he looks at the fish in the plastic bags.*

And I need a few things at the supermarket.

JOHN: Excuse me…

NIGEL: [*whispering*] How much do you need?

He holds out the money; she takes another twenty.

JOHN: What's wrong with these fish?

NIGEL: There's nothing wrong with them.

JOHN: Then why are they…?

MRS SPENCE: They're waiting for the right temperature. My son knows all about it. He can explain it to you.

NIGEL: [*quickly*] But he's not here.

MRS SPENCE: Neither is his mother.

    Pause.

JOHN: Should they be?

NIGEL: Not really, no.

JOHN: You can take care of the fish without them?

NIGEL: Yes, we're perfectly capable. Is there anything else I can help you with?

JOHN: Could you recommend a good place to eat? I'm starving.

NIGEL: Well…

JOHN: I probably shouldn't be asking you. But there's no-one else.

NIGEL: Why shouldn't you ask me?

JOHN: You don't seem to have a very good opinion of… anything.

NIGEL: You'd like to eat somewhere local?

JOHN: If possible.

NIGEL: Difficult.

JOHN: I thought it might be.

MRS SPENCE: I can recommend a place. A very nice place. The Pandora.

NIGEL: The Pandora's closed. It's been closed for months.

MRS SPENCE: They do a very good onion tart, and a lovely crepe.

NIGEL: It's closed.

JOHN: Is it a French restaurant?

NIGEL: It was.

MRS SPENCE: The lady who runs the place is called Monique.

NIGEL: She's gone.

MRS SPENCE: But she doesn't have an accent.

NIGEL: She's moved. She moved to… to…

JOHN: Paris?

NIGEL: Geelong, I think.

MRS SPENCE: How do you know?

NIGEL: I used to have the occasional conversation with her.

MRS SPENCE: What about?

NIGEL: I don't remember.

MRS SPENCE: Why won't you tell me?

NIGEL: Because I don't remember. Why should I tell you?

MRS SPENCE: I'm always interested to hear about your friends.

NIGEL: She wasn't a friend of mine.

MRS SPENCE: Why not? She was a perfectly charming woman. You don't have enough friends. You seem to have the social life of a badger.

NIGEL: A badger?

MRS SPENCE: They're very solitary creatures, so I've heard.

NIGEL: Where did you hear this?

JOHN: I'm sorry, excuse me, I don't mean to interrupt, but—

NIGEL: I think you've been misinformed.

MRS SPENCE: [*to* JOHN] Do you know anything about badgers?

JOHN: Nothing apart from the fact that they're related to the ferret and the weasel. There is some recent genetic evidence that suggests certain types of badger may be related to the skunk, but I'm sceptical.

NIGEL: Are you a zoologist?

JOHN: No.

MRS SPENCE: Are they solitary creatures?

JOHN: Some are, some aren't.

MRS SPENCE: [*to* NIGEL] See, I told you so.

NIGEL: How does he know? He's just admitted that he's not a zoologist.

JOHN: Excuse me, but can I—?

MRS SPENCE: He doesn't have to be a zoologist.

JOHN: Can I just ask—?

NIGEL: He's got nothing to back up his opinions about badgers, that's all I'm saying.

JOHN: Can I just ask if there's another restaurant anywhere nearby?

NIGEL: No, there isn't.

JOHN: I see.

NIGEL: What were you thinking of eating?

JOHN: Whatever I could find.

NIGEL: Because I could do you something on the hotplate if you like.

JOHN: Thanks, really, but—

NIGEL: I was going to have some sausages.

> *Pause.*

JOHN: Sausages?

NIGEL: With fried tomatoes and onion.

JOHN: Are you sure? I mean, after the incident with the toast…

NIGEL: That was an aberration.

MRS SPENCE: What incident?

NIGEL: [*to* MRS SPENCE] It's of no importance. [*To* JOHN] I'm perfectly
    capable of cooking a few sausages.

MRS SPENCE: I'd love a sausage.

NIGEL: Oh. Then I don't know if I've got enough.

MRS SPENCE: I'd just want the one.

NIGEL: [*to* JOHN] How many would you like?

JOHN: Three?

NIGEL: That leaves two for me. I've only got half a dozen.

JOHN: We could have two and a half each.

NIGEL: Two and a half? That doesn't seem right. You can't have half a
    sausage. You have a whole sausage or no sausage at all.

JOHN: I'd settle for two.

NIGEL: Are you sure? I don't want to take food out of your mouth.

JOHN: Two would be perfectly okay.

MRS SPENCE: And one for me.

NIGEL: Well… that all seems fair enough.

      JOHN *goes to the desk.*

JOHN: How much?

NIGEL: Ten dollars.

JOHN: Ten…

NIGEL: With tomatoes and onions.

JOHN: Very reasonable. I suppose there's nothing to drink, alcohol-wise?

NIGEL: No.

JOHN: I didn't think so. I've got a bottle of wine in my suitcase. Would it
    be alright if I…?

NIGEL: Why not?

JOHN: [*to* MRS SPENCE] Wine and sausages, eh? Very classy…

MRS SPENCE: Lovely. This is nice.

NIGEL: I'll warm up the hotplate. It takes a while. We should be eating in about half an hour.

JOHN: I'll get the wine.

> NIGEL *goes into the office.*

> JOHN *makes for the elevator, thinks better of it, opens the door to the stairs.*

MRS SPENCE: A hotel lobby is a strange kind of place, isn't it?

> JOHN *stops and turns to* MRS SPENCE.

When you're in one you're either checking in or checking out… not yet properly arrived, or not entirely departed. You're in between. A person is always somewhere, but in a hotel lobby… where are you exactly?

JOHN: I've no idea.

MRS SPENCE: Neither have I.

> JOHN *turns and heads up the stairs, the door closing behind him.*

> *We hear him climbing the stairs.* MRS SPENCE *listens; she looks up. We hear John's footsteps as he walks along the upstairs hallway. He reaches his room; we hear his key turning in the lock. The door opens; the door shuts.*

> *Pause.*

> MRS SPENCE *gets up, goes to the desk and calls.*

Nigel?

NIGEL: [*off*] Yes?

MRS SPENCE: I think I will have a little lie-down.

NIGEL: [*off*] Okay.

MRS SPENCE: You can give me a call when the food's ready. The phones are working, aren't they?

NIGEL: [*off*] Yes.

MRS SPENCE: I'll come straight down when you call. I'm just very tired.

NIGEL: [*off*] Okay.

> *She moves towards the fish tank.*

MRS SPENCE: And, dear…

NIGEL: [*off*] Yes?

MRS SPENCE: Please do something about these poor fish. They've been in those plastic bags all morning. They're looking very claustrophobic.

She waits, but there is no response. She shrugs, goes to the elevator and presses the button.

The doors open with a bright 'ting'.

She steps inside, presses the button for the third floor.

[*Smiling*] This is all turning out quite nicely.

The doors close.

Pause.

Faintly at first, we hear MRS SPENCE *pounding on the doors of the elevator.*

Pause.

NIGEL *comes out of the office holding a string of sausages, a tea towel slung over his shoulder. He looks towards the elevator.*

The pounding grows louder.

NIGEL: Well, that was bound to happen, wasn't it?

The pounding continues as the lights fade to black.

SCENE FOUR

Lights rise on the balcony, right.

Night.

TOM *and* ELLEN.

TOM: Not much of a view, is it?

He looks down over the edge of the balcony; then he looks up.

This must be some kind of ventilation shaft.

ELLEN: Why are we here?

TOM: We needed to get away.

ELLEN: From what?

TOM: The usual.

ELLEN: The usual what?

TOM: We've already talked about this, haven't we?

ELLEN: I'm here because it's what we decided to do, but I'm not sure why we decided to do it.

TOM: If you didn't want to do it you should have said so.

ELLEN: I don't know what we're doing.

Pause.

TOM: The first time I ever saw you was in the playground. I pushed you off the swings. Do you remember that?

ELLEN: You were a brute.

TOM: I thought you were pretty.

ELLEN: Is that why you pushed me?

TOM: Maybe.

ELLEN: And maybe you just wanted to use the swing.

TOM: Probably.

Pause.

ELLEN: So?

TOM: We've been together since we were kids.

ELLEN: I know that.

TOM: But we never…

Pause.

ELLEN: What?

TOM: We never met.

ELLEN: Never met?

TOM: No.

ELLEN: What are you talking about?

TOM: We've always been together.

ELLEN: No we haven't.

TOM: It seems that way.

ELLEN: No it doesn't.

TOM: There should have been a moment, a moment that you and I can remember, when you and I… collided… the moment when I met you and you met me and everything was suddenly different.

ELLEN: What was different?

TOM: Everything. Life.

ELLEN: Maybe things don't happen like that. People just—

TOM: They do happen like that. They have to.

ELLEN: Do they?

TOM: Yes.

> *Pause.*

ELLEN: Are you bored with…?

> *Pause.*

TOM: What?

ELLEN: With everything. Me?

TOM: Of course not.

ELLEN: Don't lie, please.

TOM: I'm not lying.

ELLEN: Sometimes you say things that aren't true.

TOM: I don't.

ELLEN: You say them because you want them to be true.

TOM: I don't know what you're talking about.

ELLEN: That's a lie.

> TOM *moves away from* ELLEN, *turning his back to her.*
>
> *After a pause:*

TOM: Don't look at me that way.

ELLEN: How am I looking at you?

TOM: The way you look at me.

ELLEN: I like looking at you.

> *She moves close to him; he turns to her.*

TOM: We should go out somewhere tonight.

ELLEN: Where would you like to go?

TOM: Some place… where we can pretend we don't know each other.

ELLEN: Why do you want to do that?

TOM: Imagine if I didn't know you. Can you do that?

> ELLEN *doesn't respond.*

TOM *embraces her.*

ELLEN: I don't want to play this game.

TOM: It isn't a game.

ELLEN: What is it?

TOM: I don't know.

      ELLEN *releases herself from* TOM*'s embrace.*

ELLEN: Are you sure?

TOM: Yes, I'm sure.

ELLEN: I'm not.

TOM: Please, Ellen… [*Pause.*] Please…

      Pause.

ELLEN: I'll change my clothes.

      She goes into their room; TOM *remains on the balcony.*

      Lights fade and rise on the balcony, left.

      ALICE *and* ROY.

      Pause.

ROY: You haven't answered my question.

ALICE: Can we really do what you're saying we can?

      Pause.

ROY: What's life given us? You were happy once, so was I. Neither of us are happy anymore. Is that all there is to it?

      ALICE *doesn't respond.*

Why can't we be who we want each other to be? [*Pause.*] I like… observing people. Sometimes I make up stories about them. I don't know why. It's a habit of mine. I don't know if the stories are true or not. Sometimes they might be. [*Pause.*] Why can't we make up stories about ourselves? What's to stop us?

ALICE: But what we know—

ROY: What we know doesn't matter. Sometimes I think that all I know about myself is what I've lost.

ALICE: I've thought that too. I've tried not to.

ROY: I can't go on like that.

ALICE: Do we have a choice?

ROY: Alice, I feel worn down to a shadow. I'm… fading. And I've stopped putting up a struggle. My life just goes on day after day, but it goes on without me in it. I'm simply watching myself. I don't often like what I see. [*Pause*.] Can't I be him? Can't you be her?

    Pause.

ALICE: He wasn't always kind. He was angry, often. And often hurt. [*Pause*.] The world is filled with sharp corners, with spikes and edges. It makes me wince to think of how many ways a person can be hurt by the world, hurt and not know they have been, or know they have been and not know how.

    Pause.

ROY: Am I like him at all?

ALICE: You don't have to be. Am I like her?

ROY: I can tell myself you are, and you will be.

    ROY *takes* ALICE*'s hand in his.*

We can be whoever we want to be.

ALICE: You have a son, a life… you can't change that.

ROY: I don't have to change anything. I'll go home, and I'll tell my son what's happened. When he was younger he was interested in my life. He used to ask me all kinds of questions. I couldn't think what else to do but to tell him the truth. I'll tell him that I've found Alice again, after all these years. He'll probably be pleased for me. He likes to be pleased for other people, he's generous that way.

ALICE: I thought he drove you to distraction.

ROY: He does. But not all the time. He has that gift… he can be forgiven.

    Pause.

ALICE: So… you'll go home tonight?

ROY: Yes. I don't want us to… to… begin here, not in this place.

ALICE: What shall we do?

ROY: We'll meet tomorrow. There's a café I haven't been to for years, in fact I've avoided it. It's where we first met. I'm sure you remember it.

ALICE: I suppose I must.

ROY: I'll help you, will I?

ALICE: Please.

ROY: It's in Market Lane. It isn't very large or flash, there are only a few tables, but the food is wonderful. I was sitting near the window and I was about to pay my bill when you walked in…

ALICE: What was I wearing?

ROY: I remember exactly.

ALICE: Tell me.

> *Lights fade on the balcony.*
>
> *Lights rise on the lobby.*
>
> *The fish are swimming in the fish tank.*
>
> *Empty dinner plates, an empty wine bottle and glasses litter the coffee table.*
>
> NIGEL *is standing on the reception desk, replacing an overhead light bulb. He isn't quite tall enough to reach the light fitting; he stands on his toes, teetering on the brink of falling. He successfully replaces the light bulb.*
>
> *The revolving door spins and* JOHN *stumbles in, dishevelled and breathless. He moves directly to* NIGEL.

JOHN: It's happened again.

NIGEL: Has it? What?

JOHN: I can't leave. I've been out there for hours. Every street looks the same, the same walls, same windows, same doorways. I thought if I just walked in a straight line for long enough I'd end up somewhere else. Anywhere else would do. But there are no straight lines. I turned… and I turned again. I thought I was getting somewhere. It was incredible. I really thought that I'd made it, I thought that I'd got out of this… maze. And then I looked up… and I was standing outside this place. Again. I didn't mean to come back here. But I came back here. Maybe I am insane. But I don't think I am. I can't possibly be sane, I know that, but does that mean I'm crazy?

NIGEL: I have no idea.

He climbs down from the desk, moves to the fish tank and stands staring at the fish.

JOHN: No matter what I do… I can't get out of this city… perhaps I can't even leave this hotel. Jesus, is that possible?

NIGEL *doesn't respond.*

JOHN *flops down in one of the armchairs.*

Maybe I should just sit here… and rot. Maybe I should do nothing. I should let fate deal with me. Maybe I shouldn't care. I'll do nothing. I've often thought that if more people did nothing we'd all be better off. Doing things is what gets people into trouble. Idleness is the state to which every human being should aspire.

He takes a long look at NIGEL, *who is still standing by the fish tank.*

You seem to have managed it.

NIGEL: What do you mean?

JOHN: [*groaning*] God, I could do with a drink. Do you really not have anything?

Pause.

NIGEL: I might have something. In case of an emergency. Is this an emergency?

JOHN: Absolutely. I think I'm becoming a tragic figure.

NIGEL *turns, goes into the office.*

JOHN *leans back and closes his eyes. He raises his voice a little, so that* NIGEL *can hear him.*

I had a life once. Do you find that hard to believe? I do…

From the office we hear the pop of a cork.

NIGEL *comes out holding a bottle of wine.*

NIGEL: Let's paint the town grey.

A sudden rumble of thunder.

Rain begins to fall.

JOHN *looks up.*

JOHN: [*quietly*] And the rain it raineth every day…

NIGEL *collects a couple of empty glasses and pours wine for himself and* JOHN. *He sits in the other armchair.*

NIGEL: Here's cheers.

They drink; JOHN *sighs with pleasure.*

JOHN: I'm like a rat in a maze. I've left the city before, and I've come back. But this time I want to leave for good. Maybe that's what's… stopping me.

NIGEL: Perhaps there's some reason that you… are yet to understand. Something that you've forgotten? Something… hidden?

JOHN: Have you dabbled in psychology?

NIGEL: I've taken an interest.

JOHN: In what capacity?

NIGEL: As a layman.

JOHN: Not as a patient?

NIGEL: What are you suggesting?

JOHN: It seems to me that those who would best know the failures and successes of the mental arts are those who have suffered the injuries of their practice.

NIGEL: The mental arts… that's a very nice way of putting it.

JOHN: I'm glad you enjoyed it.

NIGEL: But no, I am not an expert and don't pretend to be.

JOHN: What do you pretend to be?

NIGEL: Myself.

JOHN: Oh dear. Then there's nothing to be done for you.

They both drink.

God, this is good wine, isn't it?

NIGEL: It flavours the brain.

JOHN: What a lovely way of putting it.

He empties his glass; NIGEL *fills it again.*

JOHN *stands up and moves to the fish tank; he gazes at the fish.*

Apparently fish have very short memories. It's only a matter of seconds. Every time they swim to this end of the tank [*moving to one end of the tank*] they've already forgotten [*moving to the other end of the tank*] this end. So when they turn around and swim back, it's all new to them. That little journey from one end of the tank to the other is always the first journey, into an unknown future. Except for a few short seconds of memory they live entirely in the present. For a fish there is only now. Isn't that remarkable? A fish can't regret anything, or hope for anything. They must be nature's most fortunate creations.

NIGEL: I don't think mosquitoes hope for anything either. Or tapeworms.

JOHN: Do you think it's only humans who do?

NIGEL: You're entering rather complicated terrain when you ask questions like that. You're going to have to consider the whole idea of what it means to be conscious. There are some who would argue that memory itself is consciousness.

> *Pause.*

JOHN: You're rather lucid for a hotel clerk.

NIGEL: What are they usually?

JOHN: I've found them of very little substance.

NIGEL: But do you think it appropriate or necessary that a hotel clerk would reveal to you the full extent of their character? I mean, in the process of signing the register and collecting your key, is there any genuine opportunity for the hotel clerk to reveal to you anything other than their ability to perform the immediate function that they are employed to perform? And if such an opportunity existed within the brief moments of your rather perfunctory transaction with them, would there be any point in their doing so? To what end? For whose benefit?

> JOHN *approaches and sits in the armchair.*

JOHN: You're a very interesting person.

NIGEL: For a hotel clerk…

JOHN: Although you're not really a hotel clerk, are you?

NIGEL: What am I, really?

JOHN: You're the future owner of this hotel when your mother… passes on.

NIGEL: Are you a detective?

JOHN: No, just a keen observer of people.

NIGEL: I would never have guessed.

JOHN: So the hotel will be yours.

NIGEL: I'll sell it before my mother's body's in the ground.

JOHN: She wouldn't prefer cremation?

NIGEL: She wants to lie beside my father, who had a fear of fire.

JOHN: During our recent dinner I was led to believe, by your mother in fact, that your father was still with us.

NIGEL: [*sighing*] Yes. He's still with her, now and then, when she forgets that he's dead. He used to wander off, he'd be gone for days, and then he'd turn up again. She sometimes thinks he's still at it.

JOHN: Where had he been?

NIGEL: 'Elsewhere' was the only explanation he would ever give.

JOHN: And did he always return... as he had been?

NIGEL: Completely unchanged. He was, if it's possible, even more like himself than before. [*Pause.*] When he was gone, my mother and I carried on as usual. We set the table for three, she laid out his clothes, she sat alone in the living room perfectly content, as if he was there sitting beside her. You could say that his life, as it were, went on without him. And then he would step back into it, as you might step into a familiar pair of trousers.

JOHN: What a remarkable man.

NIGEL: It depends on what you mean by remarkable. I thought he was a complete pain in the arse.

>   *Pause.*

JOHN: I've... wandered off. But I can't seem to get very far.

NIGEL: There's an art to it.

JOHN: To what?

NIGEL: Escape.

>   *They raise their glasses and drink.*

>   *Pause.*

>   So... there's no-one else? No... complications?

JOHN: There was someone else. There isn't anymore. [*He empties his glass again. He stands up and moves around the lobby.*] Some people are ablaze. They burn the air, they burn up all the oxygen. You can't breathe when you're near them. You have to watch them from a distance. She was like that. [*Pause.*] I wanted love to make me happy. When it didn't I pretended that it did. No-one wants to face the fact that love can become... a hollow thing, that nothing can fill except... grief, maybe. [*Pause.*] After we divorced I didn't see her for a long time. When I finally did it was only by accident. I saw her on a street corner, just standing there. I walked up to her and said hello and she kissed my cheek, as if we'd been together only yesterday. We talked. We didn't talk about the past. We didn't talk about the future. We had the kind of conversation that's meant to be forgotten, that simply passes the time, a certain amount of time, an appropriate time, a polite time. [*Pause.*] She smiled at me when we said goodbye and touched my face. I wore that touch all the way home. [*Pause.*] We meet now and then. I don't know why. Perhaps we shouldn't. My life stops when I'm with her. [*He returns to the armchair and sits down.*] I don't know what my life means anymore. I'm just caught in it, exhausted by it. My life just seems to go on, but... without me in it.

The elevator doors open with a bright 'ting'.

JOHN *and* NIGEL *look around.*

The doors open; the elevator is empty.

After a short pause, we hear the sound of footsteps coming down the stairs.

MRS SPENCE *enters the lobby.*

NIGEL: Hello, Mum.

MRS SPENCE: Hello, dear.

NIGEL *goes to the elevator and looks in. He reaches in and presses a button; nothing happens. He presses the button again; nothing. He steps inside the elevator, pressing buttons. The doors finally begin to close.* NIGEL *leaps out before they shut completely.*

During all of this, MRS SPENCE *has gone over to* JOHN *and sits in the armchair.*

Good evening.

JOHN: Hello again, how are you?

MRS SPENCE: I became quite light-headed after eating that sausage.

JOHN: Did you?

MRS SPENCE: I had to have a lie-down in my room.

JOHN: You did look a little pale.

MRS SPENCE: They had no ill effect on you?

JOHN: I have an iron constitution.

MRS SPENCE: I used to have, but it's all a little rusty now. I'm quite old you know, almost mummified. [*She looks at* NIGEL.] It's like an empty tomb upstairs, Nigel.

NIGEL: It is the off-season.

MRS SPENCE: When is the on-season?

> NIGEL *finds an empty glass and pours his mother the last of the wine, handing it to her.*

NIGEL: I'll get another bottle. Then I'll explain it to you.

> *He goes back into the office.*

MRS SPENCE: [*to* JOHN, *sipping her wine*] This is very pleasant, isn't it?

JOHN: You have a very… cheery disposition.

MRS SPENCE: I don't feel very cheery. Just the opposite. Perhaps it was that sausage… [*Pause.*] Nigel's given me money for a taxi home. I'm not supposed to be here. There's some chap, I don't know who he is, who mustn't see me. It's quite exciting. Although I've no idea what's going on. I very seldom do these days. There are moments when I'd like to be more… aware of what's happening around me, but most of what's happening doesn't concern me, so I can't complain.

> *We hear the pop of a cork from the office.*

> MRS SPENCE *sighs; she looks around the lobby.*

This place, this, let's be honest, this dump, once used to be my pride and joy. It isn't anymore; it's just a… what's that bird that hung around that poor chap's neck? He was a sailor. Do you know who I mean?

JOHN: The Ancient Mariner.

MRS SPENCE: That's him.

JOHN: It was an albatross that hung around his neck.

MRS SPENCE: It was, yes, that's what it was.

JOHN: He had to tell the same story, over and over again, about the albatross.

MRS SPENCE: That's what this place is, my albatross. I should change the name. The Albatross Hotel, that has a certain ring to it. I'm only holding onto it for Nigel's sake.

She leans close to JOHN, *conspiratorially.*

[*Sotto*] Do you know anything about this chap I'm hiding from?

JOHN: He's come about the linen.

MRS SPENCE: Oh dear, has he? The linen's in a shocking state.

NIGEL *has appeared from the office holding a bottle of wine;* MRS SPENCE *turns to him.*

I'm afraid there's nothing that we can do about the linen, Nigel. We've hardly a penny to our name, have we?

NIGEL: The coffers are empty, Mum. [*He lifts the bottle of wine.*] Another drink?

MRS SPENCE: I really should be going home.

NIGEL *sits in one of the armchairs and pours himself a drink.*

When you have a home to go to, you should go there, that's what I think. Hotels are for people who have no other place to go. [*She stands up and looks around the lobby.*] I never feel quite myself when I'm here. I always feel a little lost, as if I've stepped outside of my life. I need to be where I belong. That's where we all need to be, isn't it?

JOHN *stands and approaches* MRS SPENCE. *He takes hold of her hand.*

JOHN: It's been lovely to meet you.

MRS SPENCE: Where do you belong?

JOHN: That's hard to say right now.

MRS SPENCE: Well... hopefully you'll be home soon. [*She turns away from* JOHN.] I must say goodbye to the fish.

She moves towards the tank.

JOHN: Don't tap on the glass.

MRS SPENCE: I won't. [*She stands gazing at the fish.*] They live such peaceful lives, don't they? They make no sound at all. They bother no-one. They're hardly there at all. Sometimes I feel like that.

She taps very softly on the glass.

The lights fade to black.

SCENE FIVE

Darkness.

The sound of thunder, howling wind and rain, the crackle of lightning.

The storm sounds fade as the lights rise.

NIGEL *sits in one of the armchairs, still drinking; several wine bottles litter the coffee table.*

JOHN *stands near the fish tank, a little unsteady on his feet, a glass of wine in his hand.*

With a gust of wind and rain, ELLEN *enters through the revolving door.*

She goes immediately to the desk, reaches under it, finds the bell, puts it on the desk and rings it.

NIGEL: [*moving to the desk*] Please don't do that.

NIGEL *puts the bell back under the counter.*

ELLEN: Can I have my key please?

NIGEL: Certainly. You're in room…

He takes the register from under the desk and opens it; runs his finger down the page, looks up at ELLEN.

What's your name again?

ELLEN *doesn't respond.*

Don't you know it? [*He turns the register to face her.*] Look at all of those names. Which one's yours? I can't remember.

ELLEN: But there's no-one here. The place is empty.

NIGEL: It is not empty.

JOHN: It's as good as empty.

NIGEL: But it isn't empty. It wouldn't be empty if there was only one person staying here, would it? Your saying it's as good as empty means nothing at all really, does it?

JOHN: Is pedantry a hobby of yours?

NIGEL: No, it's a vocation.

> TOM *staggers through the revolving doors; he holds a bunch of storm-battered flowers; he is a little drunk. He approaches the desk.*

TOM: Ellen…

ELLEN: [*to* NIGEL] This man has been following me.

TOM: Ellen… please…

ELLEN: I want you to call the police.

NIGEL: Why?

ELLEN: Because I want something done about it.

JOHN: He seems quite harmless.

> TOM *reaches the desk; he offers the flowers to* ELLEN, *who turns away.*

TOM: I am harmless. I'm a married man. I'm married to you.

ELLEN: [*to* NIGEL] Call the police.

JOHN: He is married to you.

TOM: [*to* JOHN] Thank you!

ELLEN: And who are you?

JOHN: We met, earlier, right here.

ELLEN: You've mistaken me for someone else.

TOM: He hasn't. We let him out of the elevator.

ELLEN: I've never let anyone out of an elevator.

NIGEL: Maybe you've had a memory lapse.

JOHN: That's what's happened… a temporary… what's it called?

TOM: What's what called?

NIGEL: [*pointing to the register*] Which one of these names is yours?

JOHN: [*to* ELLEN] Have you suffered a blow to the head recently?

ELLEN: What are you suggesting?

NIGEL: Perhaps you were in a car accident.

ELLEN: I don't drive.

JOHN: You might have been a passenger.

ELLEN: Whose passenger?

NIGEL: We're only trying to be helpful.

TOM: Please, Ellen, enough's enough.

ELLEN: Enough what? Why are you calling me Ellen?

JOHN: Temporary amnesia!

TOM: Ellen's your name, Ellen.

JOHN: That's what it's called.

ELLEN: What what's called?

JOHN: What's happened to you.

ELLEN: Nothing's happened to me.

TOM: Please, Ellen…

ELLEN: Why are you saying something's happened to me?

TOM: Please, let me talk to you.

JOHN: Because you don't know who you are.

ELLEN: I know perfectly well who I am.

NIGEL: Who are you?

ELLEN: That's my business.

> NIGEL *opens a drawer behind the desk, finds a room key and holds it up to* ELLEN.

NIGEL: It's this one, isn't it? Ellen…

> ELLEN *takes the key, turns quickly and heads for the stairs, the door slamming behind her.*

TOM: Ellen… please! [*Pause. He slowly turns and slumps into one of the armchairs, deflated.*] I'll wait. I'll just wait a while. Maybe later she'll… change her mind.

NIGEL: She doesn't seem like someone who changes her mind very often.

TOM: She isn't. [*Pause.*] Now what do I do?

JOHN: What happened?

TOM: It's so stupid.

NIGEL: I thought it might be.

TOM: We were playing a game, that's all.

JOHN: What game?

TOM: We pretended we didn't know each other.

NIGEL: Why?

TOM: So that we could… meet each other again.

JOHN: Who's idea was this?

TOM: Mine.

NIGEL: Yes, that is stupid.

TOM: I know it is. Now.

NIGEL: I've always considered hindsight a particularly useless facility.

JOHN: You've never found it useful?

NIGEL: I've found it irritating.

JOHN: [*to* TOM] Do you come up with these stupid ideas very often?

TOM: It's a failing of mine.

NIGEL: Every man has his failings.

JOHN: What are yours?

NIGEL: We are discussing this young man's failings, not mine.

JOHN: I'd like to hear about yours.

NIGEL: It would take me some time to think of one.

TOM: Could we please—

JOHN: I can think of several.

TOM: What should I do?

NIGEL: These stupid ideas of yours…

JOHN: They could get you into all kinds of trouble.

TOM: I am in trouble.

JOHN: [*to* NIGEL] You've seen people in trouble before, haven't you?

NIGEL: I see them constantly.

TOM: So what should I do?

JOHN: Nigel here is a very keen observer of people.

NIGEL: I am.

TOM: I could try—

JOHN: The stories he could tell you.

NIGEL: Hundreds.

JOHN: He's the one to ask for advice.

NIGEL: Certainly.

TOM: Maybe Ellen would listen to me if I—

JOHN: And he's discreet.

NIGEL: You don't have any worries there.

TOM: Maybe all I have to do is—

JOHN: Please, leave this to us.

NIGEL: You're the one who asked for advice.

TOM: I didn't think it would take this long.

JOHN: You can't hurry these things.

TOM: Maybe if I—

JOHN: Will you be quiet!

A long pause as NIGEL *and* JOHN *wonder what* TOM *should do.*

TOM: It's probably something quite obvious…

NIGEL: I often think that. It's usually a mistake.

JOHN: What you have to do… is remember what it was she first liked about you… and be like that again.

TOM: When we first met she didn't like me. I pushed her off the swing.

JOHN: What swing?

NIGEL: But she must have liked you at some point. What made her change her mind?

TOM: I've no idea. I was quite surprised myself.

JOHN: What swing?

NIGEL: You must have some idea why she liked you.

TOM: You'd have to ask her.

NIGEL: We can't very well do that, can we?

JOHN: What's this about a swing?

NIGEL: What do you think she likes about you?

Pause.

TOM: My good looks?

Pause.

JOHN: No, it probably wouldn't be that.

The revolving door spins again and ROY *staggers in, sagging under the weight of his suitcases.*

He stands breathless, still holding his suitcases; the others look at him.

ROY: I couldn't find it.

NIGEL: Couldn't find what?

ROY: The railway station.

NIGEL: I could have given you directions.

ROY: I don't need directions, I know where it is.

NIGEL: But obviously you don't.

ROY: I know where it is! But I couldn't… find it…

JOHN *approaches him.*

JOHN: Why don't you put those cases down for a start…

JOHN *has to pry* ROY's *fingers from the suitcase handles; the suitcases drop to the floor.*

ROY: I've always known where it is. But it isn't there anymore.

NIGEL: I hardly think that the railway station has moved.

ROY: Out the doors here, turn left, two blocks, turn right, turn left at the first intersection, along for one block and turn right and there it is.

NIGEL: That's right.

ROY: But it wasn't.

JOHN *leads* ROY *to one of the armchairs and sits him down.*

I don't know how long I've been walking. I don't know how I ended up back here.

TOM *extends his hand.*

TOM: I'm Tom.

ROY *shakes his hand.*

ROY: Hello. I'm Roy.

JOHN: It seems that Roy and I have the same problem.

NIGEL: He just got lost, that's all.

ROY: I did not get lost! I knew exactly where I was going.

JOHN: But you didn't get there.

ROY: No.

JOHN: You can't get out, like me.

NIGEL: Don't start all of that again.

ROY: I just want to go home.

TOM: What do you mean you can't get out?

NIGEL: Don't make him go through all that again, please.

JOHN: I've been trying to leave the city, but I can't. And now I can't seem to leave the hotel.

NIGEL: So you say.

JOHN: Yes, I do say.

> NIGEL *goes to the desk and spins the register around to face* JOHN.

NIGEL: Look at all of these names, are these people still here? They've all left. Look around, search the rooms, perhaps they're hiding under the beds… in the wardrobes… down the rat holes…

JOHN: [*to* NIGEL] When did you last leave here? When did you last go home?

NIGEL: I can go home any time I like, but I'm needed here.

JOHN: By whom?

NIGEL: The guests.

JOHN: Needed for what?

NIGEL: Whatever services need providing.

JOHN: But you don't provide any services.

NIGEL: I cooked you breakfast.

JOHN: No you didn't. You burnt it.

NIGEL: I cooked you dinner. Sausages.

JOHN: And they were very nice. But this place, as a hotel, is hopeless, a charade, a shambles.

NIGEL: I know it's a shambles. But it's a hotel.

JOHN: Only just.

NIGEL: Only just a hotel is all that it needs to be.

ROY: I think that we're straying off the point just a little.

TOM: What is the point?

JOHN: We're trapped. That's the point. I was going around in circles for days until I ended up here. And now I can't leave. This is where I was always heading, even if I didn't know it. And here I am. And here is Roy.

ROY *stands up and heads for his suitcases.*

ROY: I think I'll try again. I'm sure I'll find it this time. I must have taken a wrong turning somewhere.

JOHN *stands between* ROY *and his suitcases.*

JOHN: Don't wear yourself out, Roy, it's pointless.

NIGEL: [*looking at his watch*] The last train has long gone anyway.

ROY *looks around the lobby, deflated, defeated.*

After a pause:

ROY: Could I have a room?

NIGEL: It's seventy-five dollars, cash in advance.

ROY: I don't have any money.

NIGEL: That's tricky then, isn't it?

Pause.

ROY: Would you accept a full set of linen, queen-size, with and extra set of pillowcases thrown in?

Pause.

NIGEL: What colour?

ROY: Peach... or avocado...

Lights fade on the lobby and rise on the balcony, right.

ELLEN *appears on the balcony, drying her hair with a towel.*

Lights rise on the balcony, left.

ALICE *stands with a drink in her hand.*

She watches ELLEN.

After a pause:

ALICE: Caught in the rain?

ELLEN *looks across at* ALICE, *a little taken by surprise.*

ELLEN: Yes, I was.

ALICE: It's a beautiful night now.

ELLEN: Yes, it is.

Pause.

ALICE: Do you think that there's anything wrong with a woman drinking alone in a hotel room?

ELLEN: Nothing, except that she's drinking alone.

ALICE: But I'm the only company I enjoy, once I've had a few drinks.

ELLEN: How many have you had?

ALICE: A few.

ELLEN: And are you enjoying your own company?

ALICE: I've had an interesting day, perhaps too interesting. I feel slightly… lost.

ELLEN: I'm not at my best tonight either.

ALICE: Then I should leave you alone.

She turns to go into her room.

ELLEN: Please, don't go. I'd like someone to talk to.

ALICE: [*turning back*] But it might not be me.

ELLEN: But it might be.

ALICE: I'll stay until my glass is empty.

Pause.

ELLEN: I've had an awful night. But I'm not sure I can explain it.

ALICE: I'm already interested.

Pause.

ELLEN: I pretended not to know someone. It was a game we were playing. I thought that I wouldn't enjoy it very much, but I did, I really did, even though it started to feel like a cruel thing to do, and I kept playing, and it was suddenly like I really didn't know them, and then… [*Pause.*] It was me I didn't know. I wasn't who I thought I was… I wasn't who I was supposed to be.

ALICE: Who was the other person? Do you mind my asking?

Pause.

ELLEN: My husband.

ALICE: Oh. [*Pause.*] We all spend so much time making sure we seem to be who we're supposed to be, but inside our heads, what we think, what we feel but never say… we have such a terrible freedom.

ELLEN: Why terrible?

ALICE: We can think anything we like. We can be anyone we like. [*Pause.*] What can people know about each other? Not very much. What we're allowed to know, I suppose. [*Pause.*] We pretend that we're not, but people are really a complete mystery to one another… and to themselves. Maybe that's all that happened to you tonight. Maybe you realised that. Is that so terrible, really? I don't know.

ELLEN: It's a little frightening.

ALICE: Only a little?

> *Pause.*

ELLEN: What do you think I should do?

ALICE: I have two glasses. And you won't have to pretend not to know me.

> *Pause.*

ELLEN: What room are you?

ALICE: 207.

ELLEN: Perhaps there is something wrong with a woman drinking alone in a hotel room.

ALICE: Perhaps there is.

> ELLEN *goes back into her room.*
>
> ALICE *empties her glass.*
>
> *We hear Ellen's door open and close, her footsteps along the hallway between her room and Alice's; we hear* ELLEN*'s knock at Alice's door.* ALICE *turns and goes into her room; we hear her door open and shut.*
>
> *Lights fade on the balconies and rise on the lobby.*
>
> MRS SPENCE *stands just inside the entrance.*
>
> JOHN, NIGEL, ROY *and* TOM *stand looking at her.*

MRS SPENCE: I've never spent so long in a taxi. Round and round we went, this way and that. The driver's a lovely chap. Hasn't been in the job for that long, but did his best. He's doing a course. Hospitality. Whatever that is. Anyway, Nigel, he needs to be paid. He's waiting outside.

NIGEL: But I gave you money.

MRS SPENCE: It wasn't enough, dear. It would have been enough, if he'd been able to drive me home, but he wasn't able to. So we came back here, although I don't know how we did… all the streets looked the same. Go out and pay him dear, will you?

    NIGEL *sighs and goes outside.*

He's a good boy really. I don't know what I'd do without him. [*She looks at* JOHN, ROY *and* TOM.] We're all rather gloomy, aren't we?

JOHN: Yes, I'm afraid we are.

    She approaches TOM.

MRS SPENCE: We haven't been introduced.

TOM: I'm Tom.

MRS SPENCE: Hello, Tom, I'm Mrs Spence. [*To* JOHN] I know this gentleman, we're old friends.

JOHN: [*to* ROY] This is Mrs Spence.

ROY: [*stepping forward and offering his hand*] I'm Roy Williams. I came here about the linen.

MRS SPENCE: [*taking his hand*] Oh dear. I'm afraid that there's nothing we can do about the linen.

JOHN: It's in a shocking state.

ROY: To be perfectly honest, Mrs Spence, I really don't care about your linen at the moment, I just want to go home.

MRS SPENCE: I'd love to go home.

ROY: But there seems to be some kind of problem about leaving the hotel…

TOM: I want to go home as well… with Ellen.

MRS SPENCE: Who's Ellen?

TOM: My wife.

JOHN: She's pretending not to be at the moment.

MRS SPENCE: Oh, poor Tom.

JOHN: It would take too long to explain.

MRS SPENCE: I don't mind. I love explanations.

JOHN: I think that Tom's marital predicament is the least of our worries.

MRS SPENCE: What worries do we have?

JOHN: We can't leave the hotel. We're trapped here.

ROY: I think that's a bit of an exaggeration.

JOHN: Is it? Could you leave?

ROY: I did leave.

JOHN: But you came back. Did you mean to come back?

ROY: I lost my way, that's all.

JOHN: But how could you lose your way, a man like you, you must know every hotel in the city, every street probably. How long have you been hawking your wares in this town? How could a man like you lose his way?

TOM: This is a joke, right?

JOHN: I wish it was, believe me.

TOM: Are you trying to tell me that I can't just walk out that door and not come back?

MRS SPENCE: I've always been very glad when I've gone home… I've never liked it here.

JOHN: [to TOM] Why did you come here?

TOM: No reason. We just came here.

JOHN: Nobody comes into a hotel for no reason. Except… well…

ROY: Except what?

JOHN: Well, I did, I mean… I was blown through the door.

MRS SPENCE: It has been very windy lately.

JOHN: Yes, it has, that's true.

MRS SPENCE: I heard on the news the other day that someone was swept off the end of a pier, just blown out to sea, like a piece of paper.

ROY: We are not pieces of paper.

        NIGEL *comes back inside.*

NIGEL: God, it's windy out there. I was almost blown off the footpath.

The others all look at him.

Pause.

What?

MRS SPENCE: We were just talking about how windy it's been.

ROY: Yes.

NIGEL *goes back behind the desk.*

TOM: Ellen and I came here because I wanted... I thought if we were in a different place, a place where we were strangers, we'd see things differently, maybe we'd see ourselves differently. I thought we needed to.

NIGEL: She certainly sees you differently. She doesn't know you from Adam.

TOM: She's only saying that.

JOHN: Isn't that what you wanted her to say?

TOM: Not exactly.

NIGEL: You don't know what you want. I've seen it all before.

JOHN: Here we go...

NIGEL: People wander in here thinking all kinds of things, wanting this, wanting that, escaping one thing, looking for another, lost, miserable, confused... even hopeful sometimes. They scratch around in their rooms like mice or mope around down here like their lives have stopped and they're waiting for them to start again. It never happens. Never.

TOM *suddenly moves towards the elevator; he pushes the button.*

Please don't do that.

TOM: I'm getting Ellen now, and we're leaving.

The elevator opens with a bright 'ting'.

TOM *steps into the elevator.*

JOHN: Good luck!

TOM: [*as the doors are closing*] Thanks.

JOHN *moves to the elevator, joined by* NIGEL; *they listen at the door.*

Above, we hear the elevator arrive at the second floor; the doors open with a bright 'ting'.

NIGEL *and* JOHN *look up.*

We hear Tom's footsteps as he steps out of the elevator and walks along the hallway. He reaches his and Ellen's room; we hear the key turning in the lock. The door opens; the door shuts.

MRS SPENCE: This is exciting, isn't it? I mean, whatever's going on…

ROY *sits on one of his suitcases; he takes his handkerchief from his pocket and wipes his brow.*

ROY: I give up, I'm telling you. I've lost the plot entirely.

MRS SPENCE *approaches* ROY*; she puts her hand on his arm.*

MRS SPENCE: Would you like to show me your linen?

ROY: There's no… hope of a sale?

MRS SPENCE: I'm afraid not.

JOHN: Yes, come on, let's have a look. It might cheer us up.

JOHN *and* MRS SPENCE *sit in the armchairs.*

MRS SPENCE: Come and join us, Nigel, come on…

NIGEL *reluctantly joins them, sitting in the third armchair.*

ROY: Do you want the full presentation?

MRS SPENCE: The works.

ROY *arranges his suitcases, opens them and begins his sales pitch.*

ROY: Our range of Classic Kingsville linen is created from one hundred percent pure Egyptian cotton. The fitted sheets are generous in size and feature deep side panels.

The lights begin to fade on the lobby and rise on the balcony, left.

Promising comfort in all climates, the Classic range comes in a wide selection of up-to-the-minute designer colours, including Jamaican Sand and Wild Ochre…

ALICE *and* ELLEN *are together on Alice's balcony; they both hold drinks.*

ELLEN: I like being married. But I don't believe in it the way that my parents might have, or their parents did. I don't feel bound. I feel as if I've become exactly who I am. It's frightening sometimes, as if I'm swimming in very deep water, or flying a long way up in the sky. It's wonderful, but the water feels too deep and the sky too big and I'm not sure that I won't suddenly just... be swept away. [*Pause.*] Maybe that's what being happy is.

Pause.

ALICE: I feel happy at the moment.

ELLEN: Why? Can I ask?

Pause.

ALICE: I've become someone else, with a past I know nothing about. I'm a different Alice now, starting all over again.

ELLEN: How... wonderful?

ALICE: You'll have to keep it a secret.

ELLEN: I will. Although, to be honest, I don't know what the secret is.

ALICE: All the better for both of us.

Light rises on the balcony, right; TOM *appears.*

TOM: Ellen...

She turns to him.

Are you Ellen now?

ELLEN: This is Alice.

ALICE: [*raising her glass*] Hello.

TOM: I want us to leave, Ellen. Now.

ALICE *turns to go into her room.*

ELLEN: You don't have to go.

ALICE: No, I do. And my glass is almost empty.

ALICE *goes into her room.*

TOM: Now, Ellen, please.

ELLEN: Are you angry?

TOM: Are you?

ELLEN: I asked first.

TOM: No. Yes.

Pause.

ELLEN: So what was it like…?

TOM: You were only pretending.

ELLEN: Was I?

TOM: I hope so.

Pause.

ELLEN: For a moment… I felt like I really didn't know you.

TOM: That's how it felt for me too.

ELLEN: But I knew I loved you.

TOM: How can that be?

Pause.

ELLEN: Sometimes I look at you and I recognise your face, your hands, your voice… but at the same time they're suddenly all new to me. It's like I'm seeing you for the first time and you're… new… and so clear in my eyes. And I know I love you. Haven't you ever seen me that way?

TOM *doesn't respond.*

Tom?

TOM: I don't know what you mean.

Pause.

ELLEN: You looked so lost tonight. I don't want you to be lost without me.

TOM: Let's go home.

ELLEN: You said we never met… but who do you want to meet, Tom? Who do you want me to meet?

TOM: Let's go home, Ellen.

ELLEN: Home to what?

TOM: To the way things were, to what we had.

ELLEN: What did we have?

TOM: Each other, like always.

ELLEN: Have you heard anything I've said?

TOM: Maybe I don't want to.

ELLEN: What?

TOM: We have to leave now, right now.

ELLEN: Why?

Pause.

TOM: Because I don't know if we can.

The lights fade to black.

In the darkness we hear footsteps along the hallways upstairs, doors opening and closing, toilets flushing, footsteps up and down the stairs. These sounds fade as the next scene begins.

SCENE SIX

Roy's sample cases are still in the lobby.

A figure is curled up asleep in the sleeping bag on one of the sofas by the entrance.

MRS SPENCE *is feeding the fish. She pauses and studies them for a moment.*

MRS SPENCE: You can be Mister Shakespeare, after Nigel's old fish. And you can be… Elizabeth. That was my grandmother's name. I do hope I'm getting your genders right. Does it matter… for fish? Or are you all bi-sexual?

Footsteps are heard coming down the stairs; the door opens and ELLEN *enters looking pale and drawn. She is carrying her suitcase.*

MRS SPENCE *turns to her.*

[*Brightly*] Good morning.

ELLEN: Hello.

MRS SPENCE: I'm Nigel's mother, Mrs Spence. I haven't seen you before.

ELLEN: I haven't been here very long.

MRS SPENCE: Of course I don't see everyone, I'm not often here, I'm not actually supposed to be here, because of the man who came about the linen, but I am here at the moment, just lending a hand, because the linen doesn't seem to matter anymore.

ELLEN *stands at the desk; she puts down her suitcase.*

ELLEN: [*uncomprehending*] Oh.

MRS SPENCE *moves to behind the desk.*

MRS SPENCE: Nigel's not here at the moment, perhaps I can help you?

ELLEN: I'm checking out. [*She puts her room key on the desk.*] My husband is as well... he'll be down in a minute.

Pause.

MRS SPENCE: My dear... are you alright?

ELLEN: I'm fine.

MRS SPENCE: I'm sorry... but you look dreadful.

ELLEN: I haven't slept.

MRS SPENCE: Insomnia?

ELLEN: Something like that.

MRS SPENCE: Come, I'll show you the fish while you're waiting for your husband. I've been giving them names.

ELLEN: I'm not waiting for him.

She picks up her suitcase.

MRS SPENCE: In a hurry, are you?

ELLEN: I suppose I am.

MRS SPENCE: Well, yes, most people can't get out of here quickly enough. A hotel is a place of convenience, where everything is as it should be but nothing is as you like it.

ELLEN: That's very... observant.

MRS SPENCE: I'm very lucid in the morning. Mind you, I'm a dead loss in the afternoon. Most days I couldn't even tell you my name.

ELLEN: Mrs Spence.

MRS SPENCE: Pardon?

ELLEN: You're Mrs Spence.

MRS SPENCE: Did you like it here?

ELLEN: Well, I—

MRS SPENCE: I'm only asking because it would be good for Nigel to know. He can get very down in the dumps when business isn't going

well. It hasn't been going very well for years of course, but some
times are worse than others. What is it that you liked?

MRS SPENCE *waits expectantly.*

ELLEN: It's very… private.

MRS SPENCE: Yes, it is very private, that's because there's almost no-one
here. It's the off-season, so Nigel tells me. Anything else?

ELLEN: The room was… adequate.

MRS SPENCE: Adequate yes, adequate, we like to supply adequate rooms.
Nothing else?

ELLEN: Not that I can think of right now. I really must go…

MRS SPENCE: Private, adequate rooms. Very good. I'll tell Nigel. He will
be pleased.

ELLEN *moves towards the revolving door.*

MRS SPENCE *has turned back to the fish tank and is gazing at the
fish.*

When you leave a hotel, what do you leave behind?

ELLEN: Nothing, hopefully.

MRS SPENCE: Except your husband, perhaps…

ELLEN *stops by the door; she stares out.*

ELLEN: We're having… some time apart. It's for the best. We haven't
spent enough time apart. We've talked about it… well, we haven't
really talked about it… he doesn't want to talk about it… we didn't
have to talk about it… it was coming here that made it obvious…
being out of our element… being strangers I suppose…

She turns to MRS SPENCE, *who hasn't been listening.*

MRS SPENCE: You leave the little things you lost or threw away… bits
of paper, hairpins and buttons… the warmth of your body on the
sheets… little scraps of yourself you've forgotten before you're
even out the door. And then someone comes along and cleans it all
up. When the next guest arrives their room seems like a room that
no-one has ever stayed in before. It's as if… you were never there.

Pause.

ELLEN *turns back to the revolving doors and goes out.*

As she leaves we hear a brief burst of traffic noise; a scattering of voices; a dog barking; a whiff of music and laughter that is blown into silence by a gust of wind.

Lights fade to black

Lights rise on the balcony, left.

ALICE *and* ROY, *embracing.*

They part and turn away from each other.

After a pause:

ROY: I'm glad I didn't make it home last night.

ALICE: So am I. [*Pause.*] I thought I saw a bird, up there between those [*pointing*] two tall buildings, not much more than a shadow really, just hovering, then suddenly it was blown away by the wind. It's funny... but I'm not sure I really saw it. Some things are so fleeting...

Pause. ROY *turns to her.*

ROY: Alice...

She turns to him.

I'm not him. I'm me, as I am.

ALICE: And I'm not her either.

Pause.

ROY: We're not dishonest people, are we?

ALICE: No.

ROY: That can make things rather difficult, can't it?

ALICE: Yes, it can.

ROY: I don't mind that.

ALICE: Neither do I.

Pause.

ROY: What shall we do?

ALICE: What have we done?

Pause.

ROY: We've decided something. About ourselves. About each other.

ALICE: I'm glad we have.

ROY: So am I.

ALICE: We needn't pretend anything.

ROY: No.

> *Pause.*

ALICE: I'll pack my bags and we'll go.

ROY: Where?

ALICE: I don't know.

ROY: That café in Market Lane…

ALICE: No, we won't go there. [*Pause.*] I'd like to meet your son.

ROY: I'd like that too.

ALICE: And you can tell him the truth, the way you always have.

ROY: He'll be surprised, about you I mean. He's grown so used to me…
being alone. I have to.

ALICE: I'm tired of things I'm used to. I'm tired of hoping that I'll find
something again that I lost a long time ago. [*Pause.*] We'll leave it
all behind us, everything that we've lost… and everything we've
never had.

> *They embrace.*
>
> *Lights fade to black.*
>
> *Lights rise on the lobby.*
>
> TOM *stands by the fish tank, his suitcase on the floor beside him.*
>
> MRS SPENCE *stands beside him.*

MRS SPENCE: I've been naming the fish.

TOM: Oh, really?

MRS SPENCE: I think they should have names, don't you?

TOM: They all look pretty much the same.

MRS SPENCE: That one there… that's Elizabeth. I think it suits her.

> TOM *taps on the glass.*

TOM: Hello, Elizabeth…

> *The figure in the sleeping bag stirs and wakes; it's* JOHN. *He sits
> up.*

JOHN: Please don't do that.

> TOM *turns to* JOHN.

You should never tap on a fish tank. That tapping on the glass sends shock waves through the water that can kill a fish stone dead.

> JOHN *climbs out of the sleeping bag. Apart from his shoes, he is fully dressed, his clothes twisted around his body, his hair dishevelled.*

> *He rolls up the sleeping bag and tosses it behind the sofa, takes his shoes from under the sofa and slips them on.*

I don't know how Nigel sleeps on this thing.

MRS SPENCE: [*still looking at the fish*] Do fish sleep?

JOHN: Everything living sleeps. Sleep is the great healer.

> TOM *approaches* JOHN *and shakes his hand.*

TOM: I'm just going. I wanted to say thanks for your… help.

JOHN: So everything worked out okay?

TOM: No, it didn't.

JOHN: Oh. I'm sorry to hear that.

TOM: Don't be sorry.

JOHN: Where's… Ellen?

TOM: I don't know. She's gone.

JOHN: Gone…?

TOM: Yeah.

> *Pause.*

JOHN: So you couldn't figure out what it was she liked about you?

TOM: No. No, I couldn't.

JOHN: That's bad luck.

TOM: For who?

JOHN: For both of you.

> *The elevator doors open with a bright 'ting'.*

> NIGEL *steps out, washed, shaved and combed, wearing a clean shirt.*

> *The elevator doors close behind him.*

NIGEL: Morning, Mum.

MRS SPENCE: Good morning, Nigel.

JOHN *approaches* NIGEL.

JOHN: What did I tell you? A night's sleep in a comfortable bed works wonders.

NIGEL: I feel alright actually.

JOHN: You look terrific.

NIGEL: I think I dreamt about fish…

MRS SPENCE: I've been giving them names. Would you like to be introduced?

NIGEL: Thanks, but not just now, Mum. [*To* JOHN] How'd you go?

JOHN: The night was uneventful.

NIGEL: Did you do the toilets?

JOHN: A couple on the top floor.

NIGEL: Mousetraps?

JOHN: All checked.

NIGEL: Any victims?

JOHN: One on the second floor.

TOM *has moved to the revolving door; he stares out.*

MRS SPENCE: Are there mice?

NIGEL: Not many. There are very meagre pickings for them in this place.

MRS SPENCE: Perhaps we should get a cat…

NIGEL: Fish can get very edgy when there's a cat around.

NIGEL *puts his arm around his mother's shoulders; he looks at the fish.*

Tell me their names.

JOHN *has moved back to* TOM.

JOHN: So… what are you going to do?

TOM: I'm not sure yet.

JOHN *looks out through the door.*

JOHN: Do you think… you'll be able to leave?

TOM: Ellen had no trouble.

TOM *goes out through the revolving door;* JOHN: *watches him go.*

As he leaves we hear a brief burst of traffic noise; a scattering of voices; a dog barking; a whiff of music and laughter that is blown into silence by a gust of wind.

The elevator doors open with a bright 'ting'.

ROY *and* ALICE *step out;* ROY *carries Alice's suitcase.*

The elevator doors close behind them.

ROY: Morning all.

MRS SPENCE: Good morning.

JOHN: Morning.

ALICE: I'd like to check out please.

NIGEL *goes behind the desk.*

ALICE *hands him her key.*

ROY *puts down Alice's suitcases and approaches* JOHN; *he shakes his hand.*

ROY: Thanks.

JOHN: For what?

ROY: The breakfast.

JOHN: We didn't actually have breakfast.

ROY: It was the thought that counted. It was nice meeting you... and talking. I enjoyed that.

JOHN: So did I.

NIGEL: [*to* ALICE] So you two are... leaving together, are you?

ALICE: Yes, we are.

MRS SPENCE: Nigel, I don't think that's any of your business.

ALICE: I don't mind.

MRS SPENCE: What happens... in our private, adequate rooms is no concern of ours.

NIGEL: Up to a point, Mum.

MRS SPENCE: And I think we've reached that point, Nigel.

ALICE *turns to* MRS SPENCE.

ALICE: We haven't met.

MRS SPENCE: I'm Mrs Spence.

ALICE: Well, goodbye, Mrs Spence.

MRS SPENCE: Hello and goodbye… and nothing in between. That's a hotel lobby for you.

ALICE: *'La salle des pas perdus…'*

MRS SPENCE: I beg your pardon?

> ROY *turns away from* JOHN *and picks up Alice's suitcase.*

ROY: [*to* ALICE] Shall we go then?

JOHN: Do you think you can?

ROY: You know, I don't think we'll have any trouble.

> ALICE *moves to* ROY*'s side.*

JOHN: But are you sure? I mean—

ROY: I'm sure of it.

ALICE: [*to* JOHN] What are you talking about?

JOHN: About leaving, about not being able to leave.

ALICE: Not being able to?

ROY: It was something that happened. It won't happen now.

JOHN: I hope you're right.

ROY: [*to* ALICE] I'll tell you about it. It's funny

JOHN: Funny…?

ROY: Your face…

JOHN: What about it?

ROY: It's changed.

JOHN: Has it?

ROY: Yes, it's—

JOHN: Don't tell me.

ROY: Alright, I won't. I'll keep it to myself.

> ROY *and* ALICE *turn towards the revolving door.*

MRS SPENCE: [*to* ROY] Your sample cases…

ROY: If you don't mind… I'd like to leave those. I don't want anything to do with them anymore. Take them as a gift.

MRS SPENCE: That's very kind of you. We could certainly do with them.

NIGEL: The linen's in a shocking state.

ROY: Goodbye.

> ROY *and* ALICE *go out through the revolving door.*
>
> *As they leave we hear a brief burst of traffic noise; a scattering of voices; a dog barking; a whiff of music and laughter that is blown into silence by a gust of wind.*
>
> JOHN *moves to the revolving door and looks out.*
>
> *After a pause:*

NIGEL: Well…?

JOHN: They're hailing a taxi… they're getting in… the taxi's pulling away… they're going…

MRS SPENCE: I think I'll be going too, Nigel.

> *She gathers her coat and hat from where she left them on the sofa and puts them on.*

NIGEL: Going where?

MRS SPENCE: To visit your father.

NIGEL: Oh, God…

MRS SPENCE: It's time I did.

NIGEL: Mum…

MRS SPENCE: I know he's gone. But I know where he is.

NIGEL: What do you mean?

MRS SPENCE: He's in the cemetery, Nigel, where we put him. I can't remember exactly where we put him, but I'll find my way.

> *Pause.*

NIGEL: I know the way.

MRS SPENCE: Do you go there?

NIGEL: Now and then. When I miss him… like I used to.

> MRS SPENCE *approaches* NIGEL *and kisses his cheek.*

MRS SPENCE: You're father was a wanderer. He never let himself get stuck in one place, even with us, who he loved. The only reason I haven't sold this hotel is because of you. It's all that I've got to give you. But you seem stuck to it like a damn barnacle. Why don't you wander, Nigel? The world is a big place. Throw yourself out into the elements.

NIGEL: It's a bit too windy out there for me, Mum. I'd get blown away.

She kisses his cheek again.

MRS SPENCE: You wouldn't, you know.

She turns to JOHN *and shakes his hand.*

It's been lovely meeting you. Will we see each other again do you think?

JOHN: That's hard to say.

MRS SPENCE: You should go home.

JOHN: I don't have one.

She kisses his cheek.

MRS SPENCE: Find one. [*She moves to the fish tank and taps on the glass.*] Don't forget me.

NIGEL: Mum! Don't tap on the—

MRS SPENCE: Sorry, dear.

She moves to the revolving door.

She turns and waves, then goes out.

As she leaves we hear a brief burst of traffic noise; a scattering of voices; a dog barking; a whiff of music and laughter that is blown into silence by a gust of wind.

NIGEL *moves to the revolving door and looks out.*

After a pause:

JOHN: Well…?

NIGEL: She's at the bus stop… there's a bus arriving… she's getting on… she's gone…

Pause.

JOHN: I'll get my things.

He moves towards the elevator.

NIGEL: Are you going?

JOHN: Yes, yes, yes… everyone's going.

> *He pushes the elevator button.*
>
> *He waits; nothing happens.*

This is my chance.

> *He pushes the button again; nothing.*
>
> *He moves towards the stairs.*

NIGEL: Don't go.

> JOHN *stops and turns to* NIGEL.
>
> *Pause.*

JOHN: What?

NIGEL: Stay. [*Pause.*] For years I've watched people wash back and forth through that door… like dishwater… waiting for someone to pull the plug…

JOHN: Why would I stay?

NIGEL: There's nothing out there for you.

> *The elevator doors finally open with a bright 'ting'.*
>
> *They both look at the elevator.*

JOHN: It really should have a sign on it.

NIGEL: Certainly. [*He moves towards the desk.*] We'll put your pencil in the book.

> *He takes John's pencil from the pocket of his shirt and lays it between the open pages of the register.*
>
> *Pause.*

You can poach your own eggs. [*Pause.*] You can have a room facing the ventilation shaft if you like.

> JOHN *approaches the desk.*

JOHN: I don't know if I could afford it.

NIGEL: We can come to some kind of arrangement.

JOHN: What kind of arrangement?

NIGEL: I've no idea.

JOHN: Are you just making this up as you go?

NIGEL: Pretty much. Aren't you?

JOHN: I'd have to change my plans.

NIGEL: What plans?

Pause.

JOHN *looks slowly around the lobby.*

JOHN: This really is a sorry old place, isn't it? But I suppose it was really something... a few decades ago.

NIGEL: When I was a kid, I thought it was paradise. [*Pause.*] You can still leave, any time you like.

JOHN: But not right now... [*Pause.*] I'd love some breakfast.

NIGEL: It'll be on me.

JOHN: That's very kind of you.

NIGEL: That's my biggest failing.

JOHN: What?

NIGEL: Kindness.

JOHN: I wouldn't say it was your biggest.

NIGEL: I'll put the hotplate on. It takes a while to warm up.

NIGEL *goes into the office.*

JOHN: Nigel...

NIGEL: [*off*] Yes?

JOHN: I don't know if I'll stay.

Pause.

NIGEL: [*off*] Fair enough.

JOHN *moves to the revolving doors and looks out.*

JOHN: I'm going upstairs to clean up... change my clothes.

NIGEL: [*off*] Okay.

JOHN: Then I'll come down and... poach those eggs. I'll show you how to do it.

NIGEL: [*off*] Okay.

JOHN *moves towards the elevator and steps inside; he hesitates a moment, then pushes the button.*

The elevator doors close.

NIGEL *comes out of the office and looks up; he remains motionless.*

After a pause we hear the elevator arrive at the third floor; the doors open with a bright 'ting'. We hear John's footsteps as he steps out of the elevator and walks along the hallway. He reaches his room; we hear his key turning in the lock. The door opens; the door shuts.

The lights fade to black.

THE END

ALSO BY DANIEL KEENE AND
AVAILABLE FROM CURRENCY PRESS

All Souls

All Souls, or Day of the Dead, is when the dead return to the world of the living. One the eve of All Souls, a candle in the window allows the souls to come home to rest for a while. In the shadows of a crumbling urban landscape three couples pass under the gaze of Phillipa, an ageing homeless visionary. *All Souls* evokes a vision of our dreams and nightmares. The writing is poetic, without compromise, always perceptive and compassionate. It is a truly remarkable work from one of Australia's most gifted writers.
ISBN 978 0 86819 431 8

half & half

half & half charts the relationship between two brothers, from the beautiful but ambiguous memories of childhood, through years of estrangement, to a tentative reunion. As their kitchen garden flourishes the two brothers acknowledge the bond between them created by their mother and their mutual longing for emotional connection. At times absurd, comic and theatrical, this play cracks the code of male communication—a compelling rhythm of skipped heartbeats and sudden torrents of yearning. *half and half* explores subterranean depths before suddenly surfacing with the transforming power of love.
ISBN 978 0 86819 676 3

The Nightwatchman
Giles has lived a life amongst the rambling beauty of the old family home. Now he has gone blind, and his children Hélène and Michel have returned for a few days to move him to a secure apartment. On the outside Giles is stoic, resigned to his fate; but inside he silenty rages against the darkness. Drawn together in a garden full of echoes, the three discover tender memories of a shared past unwilling to release them.

ISBN 978 0 86819 801 9

The Serpent's Teeth
The Serpent's Teeth comprises two plays by acclaimed playwright Daniel Keene. In *Citizens*, the humanity of ordinary people is stretched to the limit as they endeavour to survive in a land torn apart from war. In *Soldiers*, although the theatre of war is far from home, its impact on family life can be just as devastating. Keene's astute and probing insight into the insidious effects of global tensions should give us all cause to reflect on the true human cost of armed conflict.

ISBN 978 0 86819 838 5

OTHER TITLES AVAILABLE IN THE MTC SERIES

Poor Boy
Matt Cameron

Jeremy Glass is an untroubled little boy until his seventh birthday, when he suddenly announces that he is really a grown man called Danny, who died some years before. How can his parents indulge his conviction that he must find his real family? And how can his eerie insistence on his true identity not resurrect painful memories for Danny's widow? With songs from Tim Finn adding expressionistic commentary on the action, Matt Cameron's *Poor Boy* delivers a supernatural story steeped in loss, anguish and redemption.

ISBN 978 0 86819 850 7

Realism
Paul Galloway

It is the summer of 1939 and in a small Moscow theatre a company of actors begins rehearsals of a new play to commemorate Stalin's sixtieth birthday. It's a tough gig, because for Soviet artists working towards the Radiant Future the old showbiz maxim 'the show must go on' is an order you can't refuse. Another opening, another show trial! *Realism* is a comedy of nerves, a backstage farce set in a pressure cooker. It's about the spirit that makes art live and the forces that want to crush it.

ISBN 978 0 86819 852 1

Rockabye
Joanna Murray-Smith

Sidney Jones, one time rock star, spent the eighties bopping from Minsk to Manchester and bonking across many rock-and-roll beds. Her agent, Alfie, believes she is perfectly poised for a comeback, but Sidney is more interested in babies. And not just any baby— Sidney want to adopt Aamy, an African orphan. In *Rockabye*, Joanna Murray-Smith tackles with her customary verve tough questions about celebrity, motherhood, and the ethics of adoption.
ISBN 978 0 86819 860 6

The Swimming Club
Hannie Rayson

Six friends. A Greek island. A summer romance. Thirty years later, would you dive in again? In 1983, when they were footloose and fancy-free, the members of the Swimming Club spent one glorious summer together working and loving on a Greek island. Now that they are middle-class, middle-aged, mid-career and mortgaged to the hilt, do they really want to carry all their burdens round the world for a reunion? And can the idealism and fervor of their youth be rekindled? Written with Hannie Rayson's characteristic wit and wisdom, *The Swimming Club* is a seductive new comedy from the writer of *Life After George* and *Inheritance*.
ISBN 978 0 86819 875 0